THE A-Z OF CLASSIC fM MUSIC

THE A-Z OF
CLASSIC *f*M
MUSIC

The perfect companion to the
world of classical music

DARREN HENLEY *&* TIM LIHOREAU

Reader's
Digest

The A-Z of Classic FM Music
This second edition published in 2011 in the United Kingdom by Vivat Direct Limited
(t/a Reader's Digest), 157 Edgware Road, London W2 2HR

First published in 2010

WRITTEN BY Darren Henley and Tim Lihoreau
The right of Darren Henley and Tim Lihoreau to be identified as the authors of this work
has been asserted by them in accordance with the Copyright, Designs and Patents Act 1998

We are committed both to the quality of our products and the service we provide
to our customers. We value your comments, so please do contact us
on 0871 351 1000 or via our website at www.readersdigest.co.uk
If you have any comments or suggestions about the content of our books,
email us at gbeditorial@readersdigest.co.uk

FOR VIVAT DIRECT
PROJECT EDITORS: Jeremy Harwood and Penny Craig
ART DIRECTOR: Anne-Marie Bulat
DESIGNER: Sailesh Patel
PROOFREADERS: Ron Pankhurst and Jon Kirkwood
INDEXER: Marie Lorimer
PREPRESS TECHNICAL MANAGER: Dean Russell
PRODUCTION CONTROLLER: Jan Bucil

COVER ILLUSTRATION AND TYPOGRAPHY: Victoria Sawdon

With thanks to: Giles Pearman, Buffie Du Pon, Vicki Simpson,
Julian Browne, Nina Hathway, Robert Harman

Printing and binding Arvato Iberia, Portugal

ISBN: 978 1 78020 003 3
BOOK CODE: 400-545-UP0000 1

CONTENTS

A WORD ABOUT CLASSIC FM

CLASSIC FM is the UK's only 100% classical music radio station. Since it began broadcasting in September 1992, the station has brought classical music to millions of people across the UK. If you've yet to discover for yourself the delights of being able to listen to classical music 24 hours a day, you can find Classic FM on 100-102 FM, online at www.classicfm.com, on Digital Radio, on Sky channel 0106, on Freesat channel 722 and on Virgin Media channel 922.

CLASSIC FM MAGAZINE is published monthly, containing full details of the station's programming, as well as the latest news and interviews from the world of classical music. A free CD accompanies each month's magazine, which is available from most newsagents.

CLASSIC FM works particularly closely with six orchestras around the UK, with the aim of encouraging new listeners to enjoy the power and passion of hearing a live orchestra playing in the concert hall. Check the station's website to find out if the Royal Scottish National Orchestra, Northern Sinfonia, the Royal Liverpool Philharmonic Orchestra, the Orchestra of Opera North, the Philharmonia Orchestra or the London Symphony Orchestra are performing near you.

CLASSIC FM has a long history of raising money for music education and therapy projects across the UK. Our charity, The Classic FM Foundation, is currently working with Nordoff Robbins to transform young lives through the power of music, by funding more than 4,000 music therapy sessions each year for children living with illness, disability, trauma or isolation.

To find out more about any part of Classic FM, log onto our website at **www.classicfm.com**

ABOUT THE AUTHORS

Darren Henley is the Managing Director of Classic FM. He joined the station shortly after its launch in 1992 as a Newsreader, becoming Programme Manager in 1999, Managing Editor in 2000, Station Manager in 2004 and Managing Director in 2006. His radio programmes have been honoured at the Sony Radio Academy Awards, the New York International Radio Festival and by the United Nations. He was named Commercial Radio Programmer of the Year in 2009. In 2011, Darren authored two independent reviews for ministers at the Department of Culture, Media and Sport and the Department for Education covering Music and Cultural Education in England. He studied politics at the University of Hull and is an Honorary Fellow of Canterbury Christ Church University, a Fellow of the Royal Society of Arts and a Companion of the Chartered Management Institute. He has written twenty books about classical music and musicians.

Tim Lihoreau is best known as the presenter of Classic FM's *More Music Breakfast* each Saturday and Sunday morning. He can also be heard across many of the station's weekday programmes sitting in for other holidaying presenters. As Classic FM's Creative Director, he works closely with Alex James in writing and producing *The A to Z of Classic FM Music* radio series, which was named Commercial Radio Programme of the Year at the Arqiva Commercial Radio Awards in 2009. Tim has won a multitude of awards for his radio writing and production on both sides of the Atlantic, as well as being the author of twelve books. With a degree in music from the University of Leeds, he was a professional pianist before moving into radio. Along with his wife, he runs three amateur choirs in his home village in Cambridgeshire and regularly plays the organ in his local church.

AUTHORS' ACKNOWLEDGEMENTS

The biggest thank you of all must go to Alex James for his expert and award-winning presentation of *The A to Z of Classic FM* Music radio programme, which you can hear every Sunday afternoon at two o'clock. We will always be grateful that, with unfailing good humour, he makes time for us each week while juggling his busy life as a writer, journalist, cheese-maker, gentleman farmer and international rock superstar. Special thanks also to Katherine Rose and Richard Dinnadge, who have led this project from the start on behalf of Reader's Digest. We are also enormously grateful to our very gracious and patient editor, Jeremy Harwood.

Enormous thanks are due to Global Radio's Founder and Executive President, Ashley Tabor, to Group Chief Executive Stephen Miron, to Director of Broadcasting Richard Park and to Chairman Charles Allen, each of whom have given unstinting encouragement and support. Thanks also to Giles Pearman, Andrea Flamini, Felix Meston, John Chittenden, Racheal Edwards and Caeshia St Paul. Among the Classic FM programming team, we must thank Nick Bailey, Jamie Beesley, Fiona Bowden, Laurence Llewelyn-Bowen, John Brunning, Stuart Campbell, Chris Chilvers, Jamie Crick, Nick Ferrari, Mark Forrest, Nigel Gayler, Howard Goodall, Matt Gubbins, Owen Hopkin, Sam Jackson, Jane Jones, Myleene Klass, David Mellor, Anne-Marie Minhall, Phil Noyce, Nicholas Owen, Emma Oxborrow, Andrea Philpotts, Rupert Reid, Oliver Melville-Smith, John Suchet, Margherita Taylor, Natalie Wheen and Andrew Wright.

FOREWORD

Albinoni was dealt a pretty useful hand in life. Son of a playing-card manufacturer, he appears to have split his time evenly between his passion for music and being a dilettante, able to live more than comfortably when he inherited money from his father's business. Not that he wasted his time, by any means. He composed a huge number of works in many different genres including more than 50 operas.

In some ways, I feel as lucky as Albinoni. Over the many months of making the Classic FM series *The A-Z of Classic FM Music* it has been the discovery of facts like these about my favourite composers that has allowed me to continue a journey that started with singing carols at junior school. My tastes have changed, as I have, although I find it hard to point to any one Damascene piece, which pierced my rock-and-roll breastplate, turning my ear towards the classical scene. For me, it has been a gradual layering of more and more new-to-me classical works, many of which I came across on the road in the car, giving me those 'pull into the lay-by and listen' moments when I simply had to stop what I was doing and let amazing music wash over me.

It's also fair to say that the more I listen, the more my classical tastes develop. To take a food analogy, it's the same thing with eating oysters. For someone who hasn't tried oysters, they are, to start with, so foreign, so unusual, it's hard to tell which bit of 'what on earth was that?' is supposed to be the part you enjoy. I didn't know what was going on the first time I had an oyster. Once I'd had about six, though, I thought there just might be something in it and once I'd had 12 they were all I could think about. Sometimes I was lost in a kind of Nirvana.

As I discovered Vivaldi and listened to him more and more, I began to think his music was perfect, impossible to beat. Now perhaps I'd say that of late Mozart or early Beethoven. Mmm, maybe Chopin, even. But then there's a whole world of beauty out there, streaked like good Stilton with rich veins of angst – Wagner, perhaps, or Puccini. Somewhere in all this I must find time for Tchaikovsky, though, who is my current favourite. Surely impossible to better?

I hope you enjoy dipping in and out of this book in the way I've enjoyed making the series. We've tried to keep everything approachable and yet engaging, hoping to solve the problems of those moments when you might hear something on Classic FM and think 'Now, just what does that mean?' As a result, no Classic FM Music stones are left unturned. We define not just the great composers (of course) but also as many of the orchestras and the artists as we can. So, here you'll find Albinoni, Bach, Delius, Elgar, Fauré, Grieg, Haydn and Mozart, plus Orff, percussion, Rachmaninov, (the great) Tchaikovsky, Verdi, Welsh National Opera and tuba. Hopefully, it will enrich your appreciation of Classic FM Music further.

Who knows, maybe the next time you find yourself near, say, Florence, in the beautiful Tuscan town of Prato, armed with the easy-to-dip-into knowledge from this book, you can look up at the impressive, horizontal lines of the cathedral and think: Zipoli!

Alex James

Alex James

INTRODUCTION

When we sat down towards the end of 2007 to plan our programmes on Classic FM for the year ahead, we dreamed up the idea of creating a genuine landmark radio series, bigger than anything else that we had previously brought to the airwaves. We wanted to develop a programme that encompassed all of the areas of classical music in one go – and we wanted to make sure that we had enough time to give each topic the attention it deserved. *The A to Z of Classic FM Music* was that programme and it had its first broadcast on 13 April 2008. At 105 episodes, each lasting for two hours, the first series alone was a mighty undertaking that would continue into the next decade.

As the series started, the respected radio critic Paul Donovan wrote in his column in *The Sunday Times* that 'It is not only the biggest show in Classic's 16-year existence, but also, I think, the biggest nonfiction series in British radio history.'

When it came to deciding on a presenter for the programme, Alex James was our first choice and we were thrilled when he agreed to take part. We believe that classical music can – and should – be a part of absolutely everyone's lives, so it was important that our new series had something for everyone. Alex is a highly celebrated musician and working with him on the programme has enabled us to take classical music to brand-new listeners, who might otherwise have never even considered tuning in. We were particularly thrilled that *The A to Z of Classic FM Music* was named Commercial Radio Programme of the Year at the 2009 Arqiva Commercial Radio Awards and that Alex was nominated as Music Broadcaster of the Year at the 2009 Sony Radio Academy Awards for his work on the series.

When Reader's Digest approached us about writing this book, we knew that we wanted to create a stand-alone work, which would be just as relevant and enjoyable for someone who had never heard the programme, as it would be for the devoted weekly listener.

Of course it has been necessary to leave out, or amalgamate, some of the topics which we covered in the 210 hours of broadcasting, but editorial selection of this kind is what Reader's Digest does best, and we believe that we have remained absolutely true to our aim of including as wide a range of composers, instruments, musical terms, ensembles and performers as possible in our alphabetical journey.

Any book like this can never be exhaustive because of the sheer amount of classical music that has been composed over the centuries, but we hope that you will agree that the next 180 pages or so reflect the greatest music ever written, which we play for you day-in and day-out on Classic FM.

Happy listening,

Darren Henley and Tim Lihoteau

A

ACADEMY OF ST. MARTIN IN THE FIELDS

Founded by the violinist Neville Marriner in 1958, the Academy of St. Martin in the Fields is based in a church of the same name just off Trafalgar Square in London. It is among the most recorded of all British orchestras, with more than 500 discs to its name and had a particularly busy period in the recording studio with the advent of CDs in the 1980s. Initially, it was formed by the musicians on a collegiate basis, without a conductor. But a couple of years after its launch, Marriner (now Sir Neville) laid down his violin and took up the conductor's baton. The orchestra varies in size from chamber to symphonic strength.

ALBENIZ, ISAAC

1860-1909

Albeniz was born in the Spanish town of Gerona. As a child, he travelled around Europe with his father, a musician who gave recitals wherever it paid him to do so. Later, Albeniz himself was something of a globetrotter, visiting musical centres as far removed as Madrid, Puerto Rico, Cuba, Leipzig, Budapest and Paris. An effortless improviser on the piano, he is best known today for his music for that instrument. Two famous names to whom he is linked are Francis Money-Coutts of the Coutts banking family, who funded Albeniz for many years, and Cecilia Sarkozy, the former wife of the French President, Nicolas Sarkozy. She is Albeniz's great granddaughter.

† **Recommended listening:**

Iberia

ALBINONI, TOMASO
1671-1751

A leading opera composer of his day, Albinoni was a fortunate man. Unlike many other musicians, his inheritance from his father's business, which manufactured playing cards and stationery, meant that he did not depend on patronage to make a living. At one time, though, he did have problems with an imposter touring Germany and passing off Albinoni's music as his own.

Albinoni's most famous work is one that was not really composed by him at all. Remo Giazotto, a 20th-century Italian musicologist, admitted he 'completed' the celebrated *Adagio in G* minor from the fragments of an otherwise lost trio sonata, though some say it is totally Giazotto's work.

† **Recommended listening:**
Oboe Concerto in D Minor, Op.9

ALLEGRI, GREGORIO
1582-1652

At the age of nine Allegri was a boy chorister at Rome's San Luigi dei Francesci. In his early twenties he was ordained as a priest, working as a composer and singer in the cathedrals of Fermo and Tivoli. In 1629, he joined the papal choir and was elected Maestro di Cappella 21 years later. His most celebrated work is his setting of the *Miserere*. The Vatican refused to allow it to be published but, in 1770, the 14-year-old Mozart wrote it down from memory after he heard a performance of it in the Sistine Chapel and so it became known to the world. Many musicologists also believe his *Sonata a Quattro* was the first piece written specifically for string quartet.

† **Recommended listening:**
Miserere

ANONYMOUS

Alongside 'Traditional', 'Anonymous' is among the most prolific of all composing credits in classical music. It covers the tunes for which, thanks to the passage of time, the composer is unknown. The further back in musical history we go, the more anonymous music there is, largely due to the fact that before printing presses were invented the dissemination of musical manuscripts depended heavily on monks copying out every single note by hand. Many tunes that we consider to be 'folk' music were never written down at all. Instead, successive generations learned the music by heart and passed it on to those who followed them.

ARRANGER

An arranger is not the person who makes sure that a group of musicians get bookings – in musical parlance, he or she is a 'fixer'. Instead, arrangers take a tune, which they may or may not have written, and make it work for a particular combination of instruments, a certain size choir, a full orchestra or even a solo performer. One great example of this is the Classic FM favourite *The Ashokan Farewell*. The original piece was a violin waltz, written by the American composer Jay Ungar. It was arranged for the Band of the Royal Marines by Major John Perkins – and it is this version that became a hit.

ASHKENAZY, VLADIMIR

1937-

Born in Russia in 1937, Ashkenazy was a pianist boy wonder, specialising in the music of Chopin. He won the second ever Tchaikovsky Piano Competition, sharing the prize with Britain's John Ogden. Ashkenazy defected from the former USSR in 1963 and settled in Britain, before moving to Switzerland. Over the years, he successfully made the leap into conducting, being appointed to a host of major positions including those of Chief Conductor of the Czech Philharmonic Orchestra and Music Director of the NHK Symphony Orchestra in Tokyo and of the European Union Youth Orchestra. He is Conductor Laureate of the Philharmonia Orchestra.

ATONAL

This term applied to music that is not written in a particular key, meaning that it is unlike almost all of the music played on Classic FM, which is written in a key and is therefore 'tonal'. You do not need to have passed your music exams to hear when the progression of a series of musical notes sounds logical and harmonious. By contrast, atonal music is 'dissonant', or jarring, with all twelve notes of the octave given equal precedence. Schoenberg is the composer who is largely credited with developing this style of composition. Be warned: this is the militant wing of classical music and listening to it can be akin to jumping off the top of a tall building without a parachute.

AUTHENTIC PERFORMANCE

This term is not a reference to the provenance of a piece of music – proving that it has been written by a certain composer. Instead, it is all about the manner in which music is played. When we say that something is an 'authentic performance' we are confirming that what we are hearing today is genuinely what the composer would have expected to hear when he wrote the work. Often, this means that the performers have to play on instruments that were around at the time the composer wrote the piece, without any modern tweaks. Top exponents of this style of performance include the Orchestre Révolutionaire et Romantique, founded by Sir John Eliot Gardiner, and Les Musiciens du Louvre, formed in 1984 by Mark Minowski.

B

BACH, CARL PHILIPP EMANUEL
1714-1788

Taught by his father, Johann Sebastian, C.P. E. Bach made his name as court harpsichordist to Frederick II of Prussia. One of the all-time great keyboard players, he wrote the definitive handbook on the subject: *The True Art of Keyboard Playing*. Later in his life, he succeeded Telemann as director of church music in Hamburg. Unlike his composer brothers, he gets his own entry here because his works bridge the gap between the Baroque period, typified by the music of his father, and the Classical period that followed, exemplified by the works of Haydn and Mozart.

† **Recommended listening:**

   Harpsichord Concerto in D minor

BACH, JOHANN SEBASTIAN
1685-1750

Among the greatest composers of all time, Johann Sebastian Bach strode like a colossus across the Baroque period of classical music. His life fell into three main sections, divided up neatly by where he was working: Weimar for nine years from when he was aged 23, Cöthen for six years from when he was 32 and Leipzig for 27 years from when he was 38 until his death.

His huge musical output is testament to the fact that Bach was undoubtedly a hard-working man. But he was also somewhat feisty, always seeming to be arguing with someone important – more often than not the person who was paying his wages. He even ended up in prison for a month when he first started working in Cöthen; he had annoyed his previous employers at Weimar so much that they ordered him to be locked up for disloyalty.

Writing church music was how Bach earned his living day-to-day, with a deluge of cantatas coming from his pen, as well as the *St. Matthew Passion*, the *St. John Passion* and the great *B Minor Mass*. Alongside this, there was a constant stream of secular instrumental music, such as the *Brandenburg Concertos*. These were written speculatively in the hope of gaining patronage and further commissions.

Curiously enough, Bach's reputation in his lifetime was nowhere near as high as it is today. When he was given his job in Leipzig, the minutes of the meeting called to appoint him read: 'Since the best men are not available, mediocre musicians must be considered.' By the end of his life, he was starting to become overshadowed by his own sons. A few decades after his death though, his music began to be rediscovered. In the first half of the 19th century, the composer Felix Mendelssohn started the ball rolling and Bach's standing has continued to grow ever since.

Bach was massively into numbers, with numerological references embedded into many of his works. He was particularly fascinated by the number 14, which is the total you arrive at if you give each of the letters in his name a numerical value depending on their place in the alphabet.

There are 53 different members of the Bach family who held positions as organists, church or town musicians. Johann Sebastian's principal composer offspring were: Carl Philipp Emanuel Bach, Johann Christian Bach, Johann Christoph Friedrich Bach and Wilhelm Friedemann Bach. As with their father, they tend to be known by their initials.

In German, the word 'Bach' means 'stream' or 'brook', which prompted Beethoven to say: 'His name should not be brook, it should be ocean!'

† **Recommended Listening:**

Toccata and Fugue in D Minor
'Sheep May Safely Graze' from *Cantata No. 208*
St. Matthew Passion
Cello Suites

🎼 J.S. BACH

1685 Born Eisenach, Germany

1695 Orphaned

1700 Becomes a chorister at St. Michael's Church, Luneburg

1703 Appointed organist at the New Church, Arnstadt and court |musician at Weimar

1707 Marries Maria Barbara Bach, his cousin

1714 Promoted to concert master at Weimar

1717 Bach becomes Kapellmeister at the court of Anhalt-Cothen. He starts composing secular keyboard and orchestral works

1720 Bach's wife dies. The next year, he marries Anna Magdalena Wielke

1723 Appointed cantor at St. Thomas' Church, Leipzig

1723-27 Completes three cycles of church cantatas, his two great passions, the *Magnificat* and other sacred works

1740 Bach's eyesight begins to fail

1748-49 Composes the *Mass in B Minor*

THE WELL-TEMPERED CLAVIER

This enormous body of work was more than 20 years in the making. It is a collection of 48 preludes and fugues to be played on a keyboard, two in each of the different major and minor keys. The first 24 were written in Bach's Cöthen period, with the second set being composed while he was in Leipzig. The 'well-tempered' in the title is a reference to 'temperament' which was a method of tuning an instrument. Bach was something of a trail-blazer in this area. In terms of the pieces themselves, the preludes are quite free-roaming, but the fugues are the exact opposite.

BALLET

Ballet is the dance form most closely connected to classical music. It primarily developed in the Renaissance courts of Italy and then in France during the reign of Louis XIV. It was around Louis XIV's time that the dance master Pierre Beauchamp, the choreographer who worked with the composer Lully, codified the five principle positions of the feet, which dancers still use today, centuries later.

From its early beginnings as a ballo, simply meaning a dance, ballet developed to become part of an operatic spectacle, usually occurring as an interlude during the opera, with especially composed music. From this integrated form, ballet gained a following and, subsequently, its independence. The Paris Opera, in particular, became a pioneering stage for stand-alone ballet.

From the 1700s onwards, ballet had its own stories, characters and, of course, music. By 1800, people were watching the sort of ballets that we still appreciate today. As well as Lully, composers such as Gluck were important in its development. Gluck applied his pioneering style, which had done much to revolutionise opera, to ballet. Much later in the 1870s, Delibes, a former Paris Opera rehearsal pianist, had big hits with *Sylvia* and *Coppélia*. Others worthy of mention include Ferdinand Herold (his *La Fille Mal Gardée*, with its popular Clog Dance, endures perhaps better than does its composer), as well as Adolphe Adam, who wrote, amongst other ballets, *Giselle* and *Le Corsaire*.

During the 19th century, the centre of the ballet world shifted, with Russia emerging as the power-house for great new works. *Swan Lake*, *Nutcracker* and *The Sleeping Beauty*, Tchaikovsky's three full-length ballets, were written between 1876 and 1892. They soon became cornerstones of the repertoire, a position they maintain to this day, often still employing the original choreography of one of the world's masters, Marius Petipa.

During the 20th century, classical ballet continued to prosper, but now alongside contemporary dance, a form which relied less on traditional *en pointe* (tiptoes) work and more on free-form, varied movement

– sometimes with music to match. When Diaghilev's Ballets Russes produced Stravinsky's major three ballets between 1910 and 1913 (*The Firebird*, *Petrushka* and *The Rite of Spring*), the company was touring Europe and the rest of the world as one of the biggest paying attractions of the day. The combination of Stravinsky's unconventional music and Nijinksy's iconoclastic choreography for *The Rite of Spring*, in particular, caused an infamous riot on the occasion of its premiere in Paris.

Today, the fruit of home-grown talents, such as Sir Kenneth Macmillan and Sir Frederick Ashton, continue to pull in crowds, although many ballet companies cast their musical nets much further, from Verdi to Vangelis.

TEN FAVOURITE BALLETS:

1	Tchaikovsky:	*Swan Lake*
2	Tchaikovsky:	*The Sleeping Beauty*
3	Tchaikovsky:	*Nutcracker*
4	Adam:	*Giselle*
5	Prokofiev:	*Romeo and Juliet*
6	Massenet:	*Manon*
7	Herold:	*La Fille Mal Gardée*
8	Prokofiev:	*Cinderella*
9	Stravinsky:	*The Rite of Spring*
10	Delibes:	*Coppélia*

BARBER, SAMUEL
1910-1981

Barber's music contrasts sharply with that of his contemporaries Schoenberg, Webern and Berg. While they championed the new atonal sound, Barber's music remained lyrical and heartfelt in style. Although still modern in feel, it achieved popular success by being massively approachable.

Barber joined Philadelphia's Curtis Institute when he was only 14 to study composition and singing. Even though he lived into his seventies, he did not produce a great amount of music. Indeed, he stopped composing altogether for the last 20 years of his life after his opera *Antony and Cleopatra*, which was commissioned to mark the opening of the new home of New York's Metropolitan Opera, received a drubbing from the critics. Probably best known for his tuneful *Adagio for Strings*, he rearranged it as an equally stunning choral work, *Agnus Dei*, in 1967.

† **Recommended Listening:**
Violin Concerto

BARCAROLLE

Barcarolles are based on the songs of Venice's gondoliers. They tend to have a gently hypnotic rhythm that goes 'dum... dum dum... dum dum... dum dum'. This is intended to suggest the gentle rocking of a gondola on a canal. The most famous barcarolle of all features in Offenbach's opera *The Tales of Hoffman* – less well known is the fact that the composer lifted it from *Die Rheinnixen*, another of his operas. Perhaps the fact that it was a goblin's song in its first incarnation might have had something to do with the earlier opera's failure.

BAROQUE PERIOD

Originally an architectural term, Baroque translates literally from the French as 'bizarre', although the Portuguese word *barocco*, meaning 'a rare, funny shaped pearl', is its true ancestor. In music, it covers the period which spans, roughly, the 150 years between 1600 and 1750.

Like its architectural counterpart, Baroque music must have seemed somewhat bizarre to the musical old guard in and around 1600. Its intricacies, particularly those of its harmonies, became more and more complex over the years. In Early music (the period preceding Baroque)

TEN FAVOURITE BAROQUE WORKS:

1   **Pachelbel:** *Canon in D*
*Pachelbel lived through the epicentre of the Baroque world
and was a close friend of the Bach family.*

2   **Allegri:** *Miserere*
written for the Sistine Chapel for Holy Week.

3   **Handel:** *Messiah*
premiered in Dublin in a music hall in Temple Bar.

4   **Vivaldi:** *Four Seasons*
a great example of Baroque's ability to depict real life.

5   **Handel:** *Zadok the Priest*
written for the coronation of George II.

6   **J.S. Bach:** *Double Violin Concerto*
the essence of Bach. Pure Baroque.

7   **J.S. Bach:** *Toccata and Fugue in D Minor*
ironically, now thought to have been composed by someone else.

8   **J.S. Bach:** *Brandenburg Concertos*
written speculatively, in hope of a fee which never came.

9   **Handel:** *Solomon*
wonderful oratorio, including parts for Harlot 1 and Harlot 2.

10   **Vivaldi:** *Gloria*
*one of Vivaldi's most popular works, despite including 'borrowings' from his own
earlier music and from Giovanni Maria Ruggieri, a contemporary Italian composer.*

harmony developed fairly slowly; its tunes possessed an inner simplicity all of their own. In the Baroque period, the notion of harmonic change just took off, while melodies became positively hyperactive (just listen to a fast movement of any of Bach's *Brandenburg Concertos* to prove this point).

Another development was music's ability to picture something of real life, whether in terms of emotions and feelings or even musical representations of landscapes and weather patterns. This change was increasingly possible because music was moving out of its traditional church setting and into the homes and palaces of the nobility. Instrumental music, so long fought by the church, was developing fast with the coming of the sonata, the suite and the concerto grosso.

Another of the shifts which occurred in the Baroque period was happening in the bass section, which saw it acting more as a musical anchor than before. Previously, the bass part, whether a vocal or instrumental one, had been just one of the parts – as free as the other parts to wander where it pleased. In the Baroque era, the bass became the cornerstone of a musical work. It was less mobile than its counterparts and therefore more able to root the harmony as it went. There are parallels with pop music here. If you take our very own Alex James in Blur or any great bass players, they play 'rooting' notes, rather than freeform tunes. This practice was firmly established in Baroque times.

The major composers of the Baroque period in terms of musical heritage are J.S. Bach, Handel and Vivaldi. However, many more, such as Corelli, Rameau, Scarlatti and Purcell, were equally important at the time.

Bartók, Béla
1881-1945

Bartók is only eclipsed by Liszt in the pantheon of all-time Hungarian greats. Alongside Zoltán Kodály, his fellow countryman, he made it his life's work to collect and preserve his country's folk music. Without their efforts, a whole body of Hungarian music might well have vanished beyond recall. Although Bartók is now thought of chiefly as a composer, he was better known as a teacher and a pianist during his lifetime. His major works include the *Concerto for Orchestra*, a one-act opera *Duke Bluebeard's Castle* and the ballet *The Miraculous Mandarin*.

† **Recommended Listening:**

Concerto for Orchestra

BASSOON

This rather large, elongated, wooden instrument sits in the woodwind section of the orchestra. In fact, it is the second-lowest of all the woodwind instruments; the lowest being its close relation, the double bassoon, which is also known as the contra-bassoon. It is a 'double reed' instrument, which means that the player makes a sound by blowing across two reeds stuck together, rather than just one on its own. In terms of the bassoon's body, it is basically two conical pieces of wood (usually maple or Brazilian rosewood), with a 'hairpin' design allowing the tube through which the sound travels to double back on itself. One of the instrument's many claims to fame is that it stars as the musical voice of the grandfather in Prokofiev's *Peter and the Wolf*.

† **Recommended Listening:**

Mozart's Bassoon Concerto

BEETHOVEN, LUDWIG VAN

1770–1827

Among the greatest and most influential of all composers, Beethoven was a late starter when compared to many of the prodigies in our A to Z, giving his first concert at the age of seven.

As a teenager, he was appointed court organist in Bonn. When he was 16, he travelled to Vienna to play for Mozart, who was 15 years older. Mozart agreed to take on the teenager as a pupil, creating one of the great 'What Ifs?' of classical music. Shortly after their meeting, Beethoven was called back home to Bonn to look after his sick mother. As a result, the lessons with Mozart never took place, but musicologists through the years have spent many hours wondering what might have transpired had they gone ahead.

Around the time of Beethoven's twentieth birthday, he met Haydn, who offered to give him lessons in Vienna. Beethoven took up the opportunity and settled in the city for the rest of his life, quickly gaining the reputation as the best keyboard player in town. Until he was 24, he tended to play for invited audiences, but then he went public with one of his own piano concertos. He found it a gruelling experience, composing right up to the last minute and suffering stomach pains in the process.

In the next few years, his confidence grew considerably and his rate of composition shot up, with piano sonatas, violin sonatas and other chamber works pouring out of him. By the time he was 29, he had completed his first symphony.

A year later, he mentioned his deafness in print for the first time, saying that it had gradually been worsening for a while. Nevertheless, he continued to compose. During his thirties, many of his greatest works received their premieres including: the *Symphonies Nos. 2* to *6*; his *Mass in C*; his *Piano Concertos Nos. 3* and *4*; and his *Violin Concerto*. His only opera, *Fidelio* had a troubled birth. It flopped in its original three-act form. So Beethoven reworked it into two acts, also changing its name from *Leonora* to the one by which it has been known ever since. He wrote no fewer than four separate versions of the overture as well.

Despite his worsening health and his by now total deafness, Beethoven continued to produce astounding new works well into his fifties. He was commissioned by London's Royal Philharmonic Society to compose his magnificent *Symphony No. 9*, which includes a setting of Schiller's poem *Ode to Joy*. It was premiered when he was aged 53, in a Viennese theatre, with a colleague standing close at hand, giving him the beat because he could not actually hear the orchestra. One of the soloists had to turn Beethoven around so that he could see that the audience were applauding.

Beethoven died at the age of 56, after making tentative sketches for a 10th Symphony.

† **Recommended Listening:**

Missa Solemnis
Piano Concerto No. 5 ('Emperor')
Piano Sonata No. 14 ('Moonlight')
Symphony No. 5
Symphony No. 6 ('Pastoral')
Violin Concerto

BEETHOVEN, LUDWIG VAN

1770	Beethoven born, Bonn, Germany
1783	First composition published
1792	Arrives in Vienna to study with Haydn
1800	Composes *First Symphony* and the *Pathétique* piano sonata
1802	Suffering from depression and the onset of deafness, writes *Heiligenstadt Testament*
1803	Composes *Second Symphony*
1805	*Third Symphony*, the *Eroica*, first performed
1807	*Fourth Symphony*
1810	*Fifth* and *Sixth Symphonies* (the latter swiftly nicknamed the *Pastoral*) both premiered at the same concert
1814	*Seventh* and *Eighth Symphonies* first performed, plus the third and final version of the opera *Fidelio*
1821	*Missa Solemnis* completed
1824	*Ninth Symphony* premiered
1824-26	Last string quartets written
1827	Beethoven dies in March

FÜR ELISE

Beethoven never married, but he fell in love with quite a few women during his life. Often his passion was unrequited. He dedicated his *Bagatelle in A minor*, which was composed in 1810, to 'Elise' – although his handwriting was so bad that musicologists believe he actually intended to dedicate it to Therese Malfatti, the wife of his doctor. His publisher misread the dedication, so one of the most famous of all Beethoven's works ended up being a musical love letter to an 'Elise' who actually never existed.

BELLINI, VINCENZO
1801-1835
Born into a close-knit Sicilian family, Bellini was said to have been singing operatic arias by the time he was 18 months old. The success of two of his early operas, *Il Pirata* and *La Straniera* propelled him to centre-stage in the Italian operatic world. He cited Rossini as a great influence on his work and, at the height of his success, was matching him in terms of financial earnings.

Bellini was one of those composers who relied on a deadline to get his creative juices flowing. He had many lovers in his life, including the famous soprano Guiditta Pasta, who created the role of Norma in Bellini's opera of the same name. Sadly, Bellini died very young. Rossini was one of the pall-bearers at his funeral in Paris.
† **Recommended Listening:**
Casta Diva from *Norma*

BERLIN PHILHARMONIC ORCHESTRA
Founded in 1882, the same year as Tottenham Hotspur Football Club, the Berliner Philharmoniker (to give it its correct name) is one of the world's greatest orchestras. Its list of principal conductors reads like a *Who's Who* of the greats, including Hans von Bülow, Richard Strauss, Wilhelm Furtwängler

and Herbert von Karajan. The latter is credited with improving the orchestra's already formidable reputation by transforming its sound and raising playing standards. Claudio Abbado succeeded von Karajan in 1989 and, 13 years later, the Liverpudlian conductor Sir Simon Rattle was appointed to the top job, having previously made his name at the City of Birmingham Symphony Orchestra. Critics and audiences the world over continue to regard both orchestra and conductor as still being at the top of their game.

BERLIOZ, HECTOR
1803-1869
Berlioz was the son of a doctor, who only grudgingly allowed him to become a musician. Initially, Berlioz followed in his father's footsteps and began medical training. But the lure of music was too strong to resist and he switched careers, studying at the Paris Conservatoire. A musical maverick, he pushed down every barrier he came across. His works were very often massive, using huge numbers of players – not just for his own pieces, but when he was putting on concerts of other people's works, too. On one legendary occasion, he conducted a performance of *Beethoven's Symphony No. 5* with no fewer than 36 double basses in the orchestra. His private life was as colourful as his musical one. He took his pursuit of lovers to extraordinary lengths, once even chasing the woman he ended up marrying dressed as a French maid.
† **Recommended Listening:**
   Symphonie Fantastique

BERNSTEIN, LEONARD
1918-1990
Born in the USA in 1918 to Russian émigré parents, Bernstein demonstrated his prodigious musical talents from a very early age. While studying music at Harvard, he met Aaron Copland, who was

to become one of the biggest influences on his music; nevertheless, it retained a style and character of its own.

Bernstein's compositions ranged from the serious and reflective, such as his *Kaddish Symphony* and *Chichester Psalms* through to his wildly successful musicals, *On The Town* and *West Side Story*. He was a virtuoso pianist and had a larger-than-life presence on stage as a conductor, most notably of the New York Philharmonic. Bernstein was also one of the first major classical music stars of the television age, presenting a long-running series of televised concerts for children. Music education remained a passion for him throughout his life and he put his naturally exuberant communication skills to great use.

† **Recommended Listening:**
  Overture to the musical *Candide*

BIZET, GEORGES
1838-1875
Bizet was studying at the Paris Conservatoire by the time he was just nine years old and he had his compositional technique well honed by the time he was 17. His biggest hit in his own lifetime was his opera *The Pearl Fishers*, which features the incredibly popular duet *Au fond du Temple Saint*.

Bizet's greatest operatic achievement was *Carmen*, the story of a gypsy girl who, eventually, is murdered outside the bullring in Seville by the lover she abandoned. It is packed full of wonderful tunes and has a violent, sexually charged story. After its premiere in 1875 proved unsuccessful, Bizet lost faith in his own work, branding it 'a definite and hopeless flop.' He retired to his bed and died from a heart attack just after its 33rd performance. Now regarded as one of the greatest operas of all time, it is still being performed in opera houses around the world getting on for a century and a half later.

† **Recommended Listening:**
  Habanera (L'amour est un oiseau rebelle) from *Carmen*

Boccherini, Luigi
1743-1805

Boccherini made a big splash in Vienna as a cellist when he was 15, going on to make a name for himself as a composer. In his early twenties, he toured around Italy and visited France and England, before settling in Madrid. The later years of his life were tough, as he struggled to make ends meet. He outlived two wives and three daughters, all of whom died tragically young. This did not help his mental state and his money worries were increased by his French publisher, who constantly forced down Boccherini's fees. He was penniless when he died at the age of 62 in a small house in Madrid. The middle finger of his left hand was said to be inflamed beyond belief – due to a lifetime's cello playing. He left two priceless Stradivari cellos in his will.

† **Recommended Listening:**

Minuet from *String Quintet in E*

Borodin, Alexander
1833-1887

The illegitimate son of a Russian prince, Borodin was a talented chemist, who opted for science over music as a full-time career. He studied medicine in St. Petersburg before eventually becoming a professor of chemistry. However, he continued to compose – he described himself as 'a Sunday composer.' His *Symphony No. 1* was eventually premiered when he was 36 years old, after which it took him roughly seven years to produce another. Its tardy appearance was not helped by his losing part of the manuscript and having to write it again. At the age of 54 he died in full national costume, dressed in full-length Cossack boots, a big red shirt and baggy blue trousers, having suffered a heart attack at a dance. He left behind an incomplete opera, *Prince Igor*, which he had worked on intermittently for 18 years. It was finished by his great friends Rimsky-Korsakov and Glazunov.

† **Recommended Listening:**

In the Steppes of Central Asia

BOURNEMOUTH SYMPHONY ORCHESTRA

Bournemouth's celebrated orchestra is not actually based in Bournemouth. Its home in fact is just down the road in Poole. It started life in the 1890s, when Sir Dan Godfrey was appointed to form a new municipal orchestra, drawing players from the Italian military band that for many years had given concerts in the town. Because of this, the orchestra still played in military uniform for the first few years of its life. It was called the Bournemouth Municipal Orchestra until 1954, when it was given its current name.

The BSO has a long pedigree of championing English music; when it celebrated its 25th anniversary, the likes of Edward Elgar sent letters of congratulation to mark its achievements in this area. Today, the BSO performs more than 130 concerts a year in venues including Poole, Bournemouth, Exeter, Portsmouth, Winchester, Weymouth, Southampton, Bristol and Basingstoke. It was notable in being the first British orchestra to appoint a female principal conductor – she was Marin Alsop, who directed the orchestra from 2002 to 2008. The dynamic young Ukrainian Kirill Karabits took over the baton at the beginning of the 2009 season.

BOYCE, WILLIAM
1711-1779

Steeped in the traditions of English choral music, William Boyce was a boy chorister at St. Paul's Cathedral. He worked as an organist in London, before becoming Composer to the Chapel Royal in 1736 and Master of the King's Musick in 1755. He was among the leading English composers of his generation, writing the music for both the funeral of George II and the coronation of George III. Boyce had to retire from his musical posts in his sixties because of his increasing deafness.

† **Recommended Listening:**

Symphony No. 4

BRAHMS, JOHANNES
1833-1897

Brahms's background was not at all well-to-do; he had to go out to work from the age of 13 to earn extra cash to help to support his family. He ended up, so it is said, playing the piano in Hamburg bars that doubled as brothels. Initially, this was the extent of his ambitions, but a meeting with Robert Schumann when Brahms was aged 20 changed all that for good. The older musician was struck not just by Brahms's keyboard talents, but also how he appeared almost to be a fully-fledged composer, without really having to try. He said that Brahms had 'sprung like Minerva fully armed from the head of the son of Cronus'.

When Schumann was committed to a lunatic asylum, Brahms moved to Düsseldorf to help Schumann's wife Clara. He soon became besotted with her. Sadly, the feeling was not reciprocated, although they remained on friendly terms until she died.

Over the years, Brahms proved himself to be masterly at all types of classical music, except opera, which he never apparently found tempting. His output of major works, however, was not fast and furious in his early years as a composer. It took him until he was 43, for instance, to produce his *Symphony No. 1*, dubbed 'Beethoven's 10th' by the critics.

At the age of 35, Brahms moved to Vienna and became good friends with Johann Strauss Jr. It heralded a particularly active creative period, during which he produced an amazing body of work, including his *Symphonies Nos. 1-4*, *Violin Concerto* and *Piano Concerto No. 2*. All of this music was Romantic and lyrical, but at the same time it was musically progressive. Some 50 years later the great modernist Schoenberg wrote an essay about how he took inspiration from Brahms and his music.

In his last decade, Brahms composed the masterly *Quintet for Clarinet* and *Strings in B minor*, but by the time Clara Schumann died in 1896, he was already physically deteriorating. He died a year later.

† **Recommended Listening:**
  Hungarian Dances

BRASS

Brass instruments do not have to be made of brass, just as woodwind instruments do not have to be made of wood. Their common feature is a cupped mouthpiece, which looks like a small fat chalice. It is plugged into one end of the instrument. When players blow into the mouthpiece, they vibrate their lips across it to produce a sound.

Heroes of the brass family include: in the higher registers, the trumpet, cornet and bugle; in the middle register, the French horn; and in the lower registers, the trombones, bass trombones and tuba. Over the years, there have been other members of the family, including the bass horn, invented in the 1970s by brass legend Robert Bobo; the natural horn, which is the devil's own instrument to master; and the ophicleide, the forerunner of the tuba, which looks a bit like a brass bassoon, only fatter.

BRITTEN, BENJAMIN
1913-1976

Britten was mentored by the composer Frank Bridge when he was just 11 years old. Later, he studied at the Royal College of Music. He became close friends with the poet W.H. Auden and they collaborated on various projects for the G.P.O. Film Unit, which produced public information films. He left Britain for the USA at the start of the Second World War, eventually returning in 1942 and moving to the Suffolk town of Aldeburgh in 1945, to set up home with the tenor, Peter Pears. They are both buried in the churchyard on the hill.

Britten founded the Aldeburgh Festival in 1948; it is still going strong today. He wrote extensively for the annual event, as well as doing an enormous amount to redefine the English opera scene, penning works such as *Peter Grimes* and *Billy Budd*, which have become a permanent part of the repertoire. His *War Requiem*

received rave reviews when it was premiered to celebrate the reconsecration of the rebuilt Coventry Cathedral in 1962.

By the 1970s, Britten's music had become increasingly simple-sounding, as if he was constantly refining his composition to the bare bones. That is not to say that the music itself was simple. His legacy is not just a large body of music, or the festival he founded, but also the way in which he managed to bridge the gap between 'the people's classical music' and 'modern classical music.' He wrote compositions that were strikingly new and modern, but they could be appreciated by real people.

† **Recommended Listening:**

Simple Symphony

BRUCH, MAX

1838-1920

Bruch composed his *Violin Concerto No. 1* when he was just 28 years old. Arguably, he spent the rest of his life trying to emulate that success. He lived his life in the shadow of Brahms, while his conservative outlook on composition may also have held him back. He wrote three operas and achieved some success with his choral works, particularly with the public in his native Germany.

Noted for his somewhat grumpy personality, Bruch spent a few bad-tempered years as Principal Conductor of the Liverpool Philharmonic Orchestra between 1880 and 1883, though, during his time on Merseyside, he did manage to produce his *Kol Nidrei*, a soulful setting for cello and orchestra of a Jewish prayer that is considered to be one of his best works. He was also in charge of the Scottish Orchestra (now Royal Scottish National Orchestra) between 1898 and 1900.

† **Recommended Listening:**

Scottish Fantasy

BRUCKNER, ANTON
1824-1896

An organist by trade, Bruckner is remembered today for his massive orchestral symphonies. Listening to one is like bathing under a waterfall of sound. Bruckner's musical style and his championship of Wagner won him no friends among the more conservative critics of his day. Although his symphonies are numbered only up to nine, he actually wrote 11 of them. He gave his *Symphony in D minor* the title '*Die Nullte*', which means that it tends to be catalogued as *No. 0*. Bizarrely, he wrote a further *Symphony in F minor* before he finally got going with his *Symphony No. 1 in C minor*. This often appears in lists of his works as *Symphony No. 00*.

† **Recommended Listening:**
  Symphony No. 4 ('The Romantic')

BUTTERWORTH, GEORGE
1885-1916

Butterworth is quite possibly the composer who could claim the title of being the least prolific in this A to Z, due to his hugely self-critical nature and to his life being tragically cut short in the First World War. His entire output numbers just 11 works, almost all of which were composed in the four years just before he joined the army. Had he lived, he would surely have been destined for greatness. He was an avid collector of folk songs, through which he became friendly with Vaughan Williams. Rather more surprisingly, he was also an enthusiastic folk dancer. He was awarded the Military Cross after his death in the trenches on the Somme. Vaughan Williams dedicated his *London Symphony* to his memory.

† **Recommended Listening:**
  The Banks of Green Willow

BYRD, WILLIAM
c.1543-1623

Along with Thomas Tallis, Byrd made up the great double-act of Elizabethan music. Byrd was organist first at Lincoln Cathedral and then, jointly with Tallis, at the Chapel Royal. Elizabeth I granted the pair the licence to print music in England. Of huge value, this gave them a monopoly over all printed music, no matter by whom it was composed. It was little wonder that when Byrd and Tallis published their *Cantiones Sacrae* in 1575, they dedicated it to the queen. Much of the detail of Byrd's life has been lost, but it is known that he was allowed to mix in the highest echelons of society despite his Roman Catholicism – a religion that at the time was definitely frowned upon in the royal court.

† **Recommended Listening:**

Ave Verum Corpus

C

CALLAS, MARIA
1923-1977

Arguably the greatest soprano of the 20th century, Callas lived her life in the glare of publicity. Incredibly talented, with an unforgettable voice and great acting ability, her glamour made her a worldwide star. American-born of Greek parents, she made her debut at La Scala, Milan, aged 27 and at the Royal Opera House in London's Covent Garden two years later, quickly becoming the most talked about soprano of her day. She looked and behaved every inch the diva and became known for her fiery temperament and a tendency to cancel her scheduled performances if she felt that she was not on top form. The myth and hype that grew up around her is second to none, but the recordings she left behind testify to her unique abilities. He fans nicknamed her La Divina – 'the divine one'.

CELESTA

This unusual instrument looks and sounds a little like a baby's piano. Invented in 1886 by Auguste Mustel, it uses metal plates struck by hammers to make its heavenly sound. As soon as he saw the new instrument in Paris, Tchaikovsky was desperate to be the first Russian to use it and it featured in *The Dance of the Sugar Plum Fairy* from his ballet *Nutcracker*. Mahler was the first composer to use the celesta in a symphony (his sixth). It is widely employed by modern-day film composers, such as John Williams, who used its magical sound in the hit tune *Hedwig's Theme* from his *Harry Potter soundtrack*.

CELLO

An abbreviation of the word violoncello, this member of the strings family is bigger than a viola and violin, but smaller than a double bass. It is played between a performer's knees, which has spawned a whole host of double-entendres down the years from conductors ('Madam, you have between your legs a fine instrument which could bring pleasure to a lot of men and all you can do is scratch it' from Sir Thomas Beecham particularly comes to mind). The composers Boccherini and Offenbach were both masterly cellists and the 20th century produced such greats as England's Jacqueline du Pré, Spain's Pablo Casals, France's Paul Tortelier and Russia's Mstislav Rostropovich. We are lucky to have a string of modern-day masters including Julian Lloyd Webber, Yo-Yo Ma and Steven Isserlis performing today.

† **Recommended Listening:**

Elgar's Cello Concerto

CHAMBER MUSIC

Chamber music is written for small groups of musicians. It has its origins in the French word *chambre* (room) and started life as music made by friends and families, keen to play for their own pleasure or the pleasure of a small audience, invited into their home.

Nowadays, chamber music is more common in the concert hall although, by its nature, these tend to be smaller halls. The most common combinations of instruments are quartets, quintets and trios. Generally, solo performance tends not to be regarded as strictly chamber music. This is partly because it lacks that one key ingredient from the origins of chamber music – namely playing with other musicians. Alongside this, how the players sound together is of the utmost importance. The musicians are playing as a team, not as a soloist with other instruments in support. Most definitions of chamber music exclude a soloist playing with an accompanist, too, although two soloists playing together would be considered chamber. Vocal music tends not to be included either.

Sometimes, chamber music is played by just one musician to a part – as opposed to a large orchestra where up to 32 musicians might be playing the same part at the same time – but this is not always the case. Nevertheless, it might be this pared-down rawness which lends chamber music, to many, a feeling of being closer to the essence of true music-making than other musical forms.

Some of the more common line-ups for chamber music include:

String quartet: two violins, viola and cello.

Clarinet quintet: clarinet plus two violins, viola and cello.

Piano trio: piano plus violin and cello.

Horn quintet: horn, violin, two violas and cello.

Sextet: various combinations occur here, including two violins, two violas and two cellos – a combination used by both Brahms and Dvošák. Beethoven, on the other hand, wrote for a string quartet plus two horns.

Other occasional ensembles include septets (seven players) and octets (groups of eight). Famous examples of the latter category were composed by Mendelssohn (all strings) and Beethoven (all wind).

TEN FAVOURITE CHAMBER WORKS:

1   Mendelssohn: *Octet*

2   Schubert: *Piano Quintet ('Trout')*

3   Mozart: *Clarinet Quintet*

4   Schubert: *String Quintet D956*

5   Borodin: *String Quartet No. 2*

6   Schubert: *String Quartet No. 14 ('Death and the Maiden')*

7   Tchaikovsky: *String Quartet No. 1*

8   Beethoven: *Grosse Fugue*

9   Mozart: *Trio for Clarinet, Viola and Piano in E flat ('Kegelstatt Trio')*

10 Saint-Saëns: *Carnival of the Animals* (*originally written for two pianos, string quintet, flute, clarinet, glockenspiel and xylophone*)

CHICAGO SYMPHONY ORCHESTRA

Established in 1891, the USA's third oldest symphony orchestra is now widely regarded as being America's greatest ensemble. Founded by Theodore Thomas, the orchestra even took his name for an eight year period following his death. The orchestra's international reputation grew to new heights between 1969 and 1991 under Music Director Sir Georg Solti. On one occasion in the 1970s, the players received so much acclaim on a triumphant tour of Europe, that they were given a ticker-tape welcome through the city on their return. Solti handed the baton on to Daniel Barenboim in 1991, with the mighty Riccardo Muti becoming only the tenth Music Director in 2006. It remains an orchestra of enviable standing on the worldwide classical music stage.

CHOPIN, FRÉDÉRIC
1810-1849

Although he was born in Poland, Chopin lived in France from the age of 21. His father was actually French but had moved to Poland, to work as a private tutor to the sons of a countess.

The youngster's musical talent, particularly at the piano, was noticed and nurtured from an early age. After studying at the Warsaw Conservatoire during his teenage years, he went on the road in 1830, giving concerts in cities as far apart as Dresden, Prague, Vienna and Stuttgart. While he was there, he heard that the Russians had marched into Warsaw, so he travelled on to Paris.

French salon society suited Chopin rather well, although he resented having to give so many piano concerts, even though they were wildly popular. He regarded himself as a composer, not a performer. He also disliked having to teach piano to members of Parisian society, even though it helped to pay the bills.

By his late twenties, Chopin was enjoying a romantic liaison with the fiery feminist novelist George Sand. They spent a famous Majorcan winter holed up in a monastery, with Chopin desperately ill and yet composing madly. It is said that his *Raindrop Prelude* came out of the trip as a direct response to the terrible weather.

In 1848, Chopin toured around England and Scotland giving concerts. His health worsened considerably and he was packed off back to Paris, where he died from tuberculosis surrounded by friends in his flat on the Place Vendôme.

Rarely can a famous composer have concentrated so much on one instrument: alongside his two piano concertos and various piano sonatas came preludes, polon-aises, waltzes, nocturnes and ballads – all composed for his great love, the piano.

† **Recommended Listening:**
Piano Concerto No. 1

CHORAL MUSIC

Choral music is, simply put, music written for a choir to perform. We can define a choir as a group of people who get together to sing, with more than one person to a part – so more than one soprano, more than one alto, and so on.

In its most common form today, a choir is in four parts: two of them male and two of them female. The females are sopranos (high) and altos (lower), the males are divided into tenors (high) and basses (lower) – often abbreviated to SATB. This is, however, only the most everyday grouping. Choral music can be sung by whatever group the composer specifies: so, SSA (an all woman set-up), SSAATTBB (two independent parts on each register), SATBSATB (two independent choirs) and the very popular (today at least) SA-Men (sopranos, altos and a mix of tenors and basses). Any setting, more or less, is possible. A good example of the approach is Allegri's *Miserere*, which is written for SSATB/SSAB: two separated choirs, one of sopranos, sopranos, altos, tenors and basses, plus one of double sopranos, altos and basses.

The choral sound developed largely in the Early and Renaissance periods of music, naturally expanded from monophonic singing (singing a one-line tune) to two monophonic lines singing in an antiphonal style (singing against each other), occasionally with a response element using a soloist.

In much the same way as concertos gradually evolved, choral singing developed through two-parts, then three-parts until it was its own fully fledged genre, of a massed body, singing with more than one person to any number of parts.

The church, the chief sponsor of music in the Early and Renaissance periods, loved choral music for its ability to set words of praise. Later, the opera house welcomed choruses with open arms.

Despite the arrival of opera, composers from Bach to Beethoven and beyond carried on writing religious choral music. It is a tradition which continues to this day in the works of composers such as John Tavener, John Rutter and Howard Goodall.

During the 19th and 20th century, the choral sound fattened up, with composers writing for bigger choirs than ever before. Mendelssohn, for example, was not averse to using a choir of 300 to sing in one of his revival performances of J.S. Bach's *St. Matthew Passion*. This is around a tenfold increase in the size of the choir from Bach's day. When it comes to scale, few have beaten a choral epic by Mahler. His *Symphony No. 8* is nicknamed the Symphony of a Thousand.

More recently, a predilection for making choral works out of instrumental ones has led to the popularity of choral versions of Elgar's *Nimrod* (*Lux Aeterna* in its choral setting) and Barber's *Adagio for Strings* (*Agnus Dei* when it is sung).

CITY OF BIRMINGHAM SYMPHONY ORCHESTRA

The Birmingham Symphony Orchestra was founded in 1920 and renamed the City of Birmingham Symphony Orchestra 28 years later. There is a long tradition of classical music in the city, with a regular music festival dating back as far as 1768. The current Music Director is the Latvian, Andris Nelsons, but it was the then

25 year-old Simon Rattle who made his name with the orchestra when he took up the baton in 1980. Under his leadership, the CBSO developed a strong reputation both at home and abroad and recorded extensively. In 1991, the city benefited from the opening of a brand new purpose-built concert venue in the heart of Birmingham. Symphony Hall remains one of the finest places anywhere to listen to classical music, with world-class acoustics.

CITY OF LONDON SINFONIA

The City of London Sinfonia was founded by the conductor Richard Hickox in 1971. He remained its Music Director until his death in 2008. The orchestra is particularly committed to the performance of the music of 20th century and contemporary British composers; it has made more than 130 recordings of them.

Although the CLS has toured as far afield as Colombia, China, Dubai, Brazil, Australia and Norway, it has specialised in taking world-class live classical music concerts to small English towns which might not otherwise experience them at all, including Ipswich, King's Lynn, High Wycombe and Chatham. It is not to be confused with either the Sinfonia of London, a studio orchestra founded by the Rank Organisation in 1955, or the London Sinfonietta, a completely separate contemporary music orchestra.

CLARINET

A member of the woodwind family, the clarinet is a single reed instrument. It originated around 1690, but the version we know today only came into being towards the middle of the 19th century. Mozart was the first composer to use the clarinet in a symphony. Clarinets come in a whole host of different varieties, so it is important to know which one is which.

The clarinet that appears in most orchestral settings is usually pitched in the key of B flat – which means that when it plays a written C in the music, it actually sounds as a B flat, one note lower. There are also a range of other clarinets in, variously, A, E flat, D and F – as well as a bass clarinet – each of which play their sounded notes differently to their written notes.

Then there is the pedal clarinet, also known as the contra-bass clarinet or the double-bass clarinet, which tends to be played only in military bands. The clarina, heckelclarina, heckelclarinette and holztrompete are musical curiosities. They are clarinet-related instruments, but only very rarely make an appearance.

† **Recommended Listening:**

  Weber's *Clarinet Concerto No.1*

CLARKE, JEREMIAH
c. 1670-1707

Clarke was a composer, who also worked as the organist at the Chapel Royal, before moving on to Winchester College and St. Paul's Cathedral. He wrote *The Prince of Denmark's March* in about 1700. Today, it is more popularly known as the *Trumpet Voluntary* and for a long time it was wrongly thought to have been composed by Henry Purcell. It remains a popular choice at wedding ceremonies, which seems unfortunate because Clarke shot himself dead after the unhappy ending of a love affair.

CLASSICAL PERIOD

The word 'Classical' means two very different things in music. Firstly, and probably originally, it is a specific period in music, generally defined as being from around 1750 to 1820, although there may be leakage around the edges. In addition, the word has come to be used as a catch-all for the music from all its fellow periods (and itself) combined.

TEN FAVOURITE CLASSICAL WORKS:

1 **Haydn:** *Symphony No. 94* – *the so-called 'Surprise Symphony' takes its name from a loud chord written to wake up post-prandial concert slumberers.*

2 **Boccherini:** *String Quintet in E* – *best-known for its use as the theme tune to* The Ladykillers.

3 **Mozart:** *Clarinet Concerto* – *a perennial favourite, the slow movement of this work came to the attention of a new generation following its use in the film* Out of Africa.

4 **Beethoven:** *Symphony No. 5* – *quite possibly the most famous opening bars of any piece in the whole of the classical music repertoire.*

5 **Spohr:** *Clarinet Concerto No. 3* – *in all, Spohr composed four clarinet concertos, of which this is the best known.*

6 **Gluck:** *The Dance of the Blessed Spirits* from *Orpheus* and *Euridice*

7 **Weber:** *Clarinet Concerto No. 1* – *something of a clarinet specialist, Weber's output for the instrument includes two concertos, a concertino, a quintet and a duo concertante.*

8 **Mozart:** *Eine Kleine Nachtmusik* – *literally 'a little night music', Mozart composed his* Serenade for Strings No. 13 in G *while he was also working on his opera* Don Giovanni.

9 **Beethoven:** *Moonlight Sonata* – *not actually given this name by the composer, his* Piano Sonata No. 14 *picked up the epithet from a critic, who said that it reminded him of the moonlight over Lake Geneva.*

10 **Haydn:** *The Creation* – *a mighty oratorio which Haydn was inspired to write after he had heard the big choral works of Handel while on a visit to England.*

So Early, Baroque, Romantic and Modern are all often simply referred to as 'classical music'. Indeed, it is something that we do in the subtitle of this book. The practice possibly started after the death of Mozart, when it became fashionable to refer to his music and others as being worthy of comparison with the classical masters. This is a little odd as the Classical period is shorter than all of the others. Nevertheless, it was classical that claimed the title of being the umbrella term. The word itself derives from the Latin word *classicus*, which has two meanings: a taxpayer or a writer of the highest class.

In terms of composers, the backbone of the Classical period is provided by Haydn, Mozart and Beethoven, but the full cast list would run into the hundreds, with composers such as Salieri and Cherubini being particularly significant. Early pioneers include C.P.E. Bach, Quantz and Gluck.

The musical changes in the Classical period came about partly as a reaction to the Baroque period that preceded it, and partly as a consequence of the linear development of musical sound. Mirroring a similar move in architecture, the musicians of the Classical period shifted from the ornate, florid and intricate to the simple, clean-lined and natural – directly reminiscent of the classicists.

CONCERTGEBOUW

Concertgebouw is Dutch for 'concert building' and the Royal Concertgebouw Orchestra has the Concertgebouw in Amsterdam as its home. The orchestra came to international prominence under its second conductor, Willem Mengelberg, who was in charge for an impressive 46 years from 1895 to 1945. He was forbidden to conduct after the Second World War because of his supposed collaboration with the Nazi occupiers of his country. More recent conductors have included Bernard Haitink and Riccardo Chailly. Mariss Jansons, regarded by some as the greatest living conductor, took over the baton in 2004. In 1988, the orchestra was granted 'Royal' status by Queen Beatrix of the Netherlands and, in 2008, The Gramophone magazine named the Concertgebouw as the top orchestra in the world.

CONCERTO

Originally a term for any music played in a concert, the Italian word concerto has now been absorbed into the English language. In modern usage, it is a musical work where a solo instrument is mixed and contrasted with the sound created by the rest of the orchestra.

Historians trace the introduction of the concerto back to the turn of the 17th century with the advent of concerti ecclesiastici (church concertos). Later came the concerto grosso (literally big concertos), which pitted a group of players against the rest of the orchestra. The Italian composer Corelli was a major force in developing this type of composition. But it was Johann Sebastian Bach who was among the first composers to create the concerto as we know it today; in his case, making the harpsichord the solo star of the show.

Mozart took the idea and ran with it, writing concertos for dozens of different instrumental groupings. As with many of the rules surrounding classical music, very few of them are hard and fast. Although concertos occur most often for solo instruments, some composers have written for larger groupings (for example Mozart's *Flute and Harp Concerto*). It is usual for concertos to be written in three movements, but this is not always the case (Brahms's *Piano Concerto No. 2* has four movements).

† **Recommended Listening:**

Grieg's *Piano Concerto*
Mendelssohn's *Violin Concerto*
Hummel's *Trumpet Concerto*
Vaughan Williams' *Tuba Concerto*

CONDUCTORS

Conductors are the gods and goddesses of the classical music world. At the highest levels, they command hefty fees (unlike the rank and file performers whom they conduct) and can tell you what they will be doing sometimes many years into the future, so great are the demands on their musical time.

Their role, musically speaking, is not just the obvious one of using their baton or hands to keep time for all the players and/or singers in front of them to see. A conductor also plays an important part as the channel of the overall interpretation of the music; they have a lot of say over how an orchestra makes a particular piece of music sound.

Some conductors choose to try to interpret a composer's wishes to the tiniest degree, hoping to bring out every nuance in the music as its writer intended it. Others prefer to simply be a channel for their own unique vision (perhaps audition would be a better word in this case) of the way the music should sound. Often this is done not just by means of time and dynamics, but via something wholly more indefinable: via the quality of the conductor's presence on the podium, via the rapport already established with the musicians, and even via mere movements and gestures of the eyes.

Historically, conductors have not always been as they are today. Early on, a mixture of the keyboard player and the leader (the head of the first violins) would jointly keep the orchestra in line. In Lully's day, a conductor would thump the floor with a broom-sized stick in order to keep time, a practice which famously led to his death when he hit his foot during his *Te Deum*, causing himself a fatal injury. Later, the composer Spohr was just one of those at the forefront of refining conducting into what it is now, championing not only use of the baton but also the addition of letters of the alphabet to scores, thus dividing them into navigable sections. The notion of the conductor as a musical interpreter originated in the 19th century, when changing attitudes to musical performance gave them far greater importance. Indeed, in many respects, composers such as Mahler and Wagner were thought of in their day as conductors first and composers second.

Great conductors of the past have included Leopold Stokowski, Wilhelm Furtwängler, Arturo Toscanini, Bruno Walter, Herbert von Karajan, Sir John Barbirolli, Sir Thomas Beecham, Sir Malcolm Sargent and Sir Adrian Boult.

Today's great conductors include:

Marin Alsop: One of the few very successful female conductors on the podium, American-born Marin Alsop made her name in the UK first as the Principal Guest Conductor of the Royal Scottish National Orchestra and of the City of London Sinfonia and, subsequently, as the Principal Conductor of the Bournemouth Symphony Orchestra. She is now Music Director of the Baltimore Symphony Orchestra.

Sir Colin Davis: Originally barred from conducting because of his supposed lack of piano skills, he was made President of the London Symphony Orchestra in 2007 after a long tenure as its chief conductor. His style has developed from one of intense raw passion to something more urbane and studied, but no less effective.

Mariss Jansons: Latvian, born in 1943, who is Music Director of the Royal Concertgebouw Orchestra. And it's in his blood too. 'As a very small boy, three years old, I was always observing… I went to my father's rehearsals. When I came home, I put my book on the table and started to conduct.'

Sir Charles Mackerras: Born in 1925, yet still winning awards for his work as both an operatic and orchestral conductor in 2009.

Vasily Petrenko: The young Russian in charge of the Royal Liverpool Philharmonic Orchestra. His vigorous and energetic style is also perfectly suited to his Principal Conductorship of the National Youth Orchestra of Great Britain.

Esa-Pekka Salonen: Born in 1958, Finnish conductor and composer, currently Chief Conductor of the Philharmonia Orchestra, who is noted for his passionate and exacting style.

COPLAND, AARON

1900-1990

Born in the USA to a Russian émigré family, Copland went to Paris at the age of 21 to learn piano with the highly influential French teacher Nadia Boulanger. Many of his early works are tough listening because he was a fan of dissonance in his twenties. He experimented with jazz and also with Mexican infusions to his music but, as time went by, he started to become more concerned with composing works that were more easily understood by the general public. Accordingly, he created barnstorming American hits, such as *El Sálon México*, *Billy the Kid*, *Rodeo* and *Fanfare for the Common Man*. Later on in life, composing became less important to him than conducting and he took every opportunity to spread the word about contemporary American classical music wherever he travelled in the world.

† **Recommended Listening:**

Appalachian Spring

COR ANGLAIS

Literally translated as 'English horn', this member of the woodwind family of instruments is neither English nor a horn. It is actually a tenor version of the oboe. According to one theory, it got its rather strange name because early tenor oboe audiences thought that it sounded like angels. The German word for 'angel' is *Engel*, but somehow the true meaning was lost in translation and it ended up being called 'English horn'. Funnily enough, we always refer to it in French, just to confuse matters further. It looks just like an oboe, except that it is slightly bigger with a bulbous bell. It has a particularly alluring sound.

† **Recommended Listening:**

Dvošák's *Symphony No. 9 ('New World')*

D

DAVIES, PETER MAXWELL
1934-

Known in the classical music world simply as 'Max', this Salford-born composer studied at the Royal Manchester (now Northern) College of Music at the same time as Harrison Birtwistle, Alexander Goehr and the pianist John Ogden, who together made up the celebrated 'Manchester Group' of musicians. After further study in Rome, he worked as Music Director at Cirencester Grammar School. He took great delight in composing specifically for youngsters and has been a staunch champion of the value of music education ever since. Then came more study and composition at Princeton and Adelaide Universities; after which he moved to Orkney in 1971. The wild and beautiful island life suited him well and has inspired many of the works he has since composed. He founded the St. Magnus Festival there in 1977. Knighted in 1987, he was appointed Master of the Queen's Music in 2004.

† **Recommended Listening:**

  Farewell to Stromness

DEBUSSY, CLAUDE
1862-1918

Rather than having formal music lessons, the young Debussy was taught by a family friend. That did not stop him from making it into the Paris Conservatoire or winning the Prix de Rome composing competition in 1884.

Debussy went through a musical turning-point in 1889, when, struck (not literally) by the gamelan that he heard at the Paris Exhibition of that year, he realised that he should strike out independently, developing his own individual style, rather than simply following in Wagner's musical slipstream. In the process, he became a true innovator.

In 1893, Debussy began to compose his opera *Pelléas et Melisande*. A year later came *Prélude à l'après-midi d'un faune*, a piece that, according to some, changed the course of classical music forever. He became friendly with the Impressionist painters of the period and is often referred to as an 'Impressionist composer'. He also worked as a music critic, using the pseudonym 'M. Croche', which translates as 'Mr. Quaver'. An interesting footnote: when he was a music student, Debussy took a summer job teaching the children of Nadezhda von Meck. She was the patron who funded Tchaikovsky on the strict understanding that they should never actually meet.

† **Recommended Listening:**

La Mer

Delibes, Léo
1836-1891

Yet another graduate of the Paris Conservatoire, Delibes was an organist as well as a composer. After leaving his student years behind him, he took up playing piano at the Théâtre Lyrique. From this point, he never looked back, particularly specialising in writing operettas and ballets for the stage. His big hits include the ballets *Coppélia* and *Sylvia* and his opera *Lakmé*. Delibes is buried in Montmartre Cemetery in Paris, alongside Degas, Dumas and other famous Ds.

† **Recommended Listening:**

The Flower Duet from *Lakmé*

DELIUS, FREDERICK
1862-1934

Delius was born in Bradford. His father wanted him to work in the family wool business, but instead he went to Florida to run an orange plantation, where he spent more time studying music than cultivating fruit. He moved to Paris, where his friends included the composers Ravel and Fauré and the painters Gauguin and Munch. Delius specialised in 'idylls' for orchestra, as well as choral works and operas. Thanks in the main to the advocacy of the conductor Sir Thomas Beecham, who became the composer's lifelong champion and friend, it is the 'idylls' that have endured the best – wonderful meanderings of orchestral colour, rich in fleeting melodies. They are also exquisitely crafted.

As a young man, Delius contracted syphilis. By the time he was in his sixties, he was crippled and practically blind. He needed an amanuensis, Eric Fenby, to help him to transfer the tunes from his head onto manuscript paper.

† **Recommended Listening:**
 On Hearing the First Cuckoo in Spring

DONIZETTI, GAETANO
1797-1848

Composers do not tend to be terribly warlike as a breed, but Donizetti was one of relatively few among their number who started off life as a soldier. It was the usual story of parental disapproval of life as a composer that propelled him to arms. He continued to write music in his spare time and was eventually discharged from the army because of the success of his opera *Zoraide di Granata*. He then made up for lost time by composing almost 30 operas in the following eight years – quite some achievement by anyone's standards. For a while, there was a school of thought that said that speed made his operas somewhat slapdash, but his work has been through something of a reassessment over the past 50 years. His greatest triumph of all is undoubtedly the tragic opera *Lucia di Lammermoor*, which received its premiere in 1832. He wrote more light-hearted masterpieces as well, notably *L'Elisir d'Amore*, *La Fille du Regiment* and *Don Pasquale*.

† **Recommended Listening:**

Una Furtiva Lagrima from *L'Elisir d'Amore*

DOUBLE BASS

Big in size and big in sound, the double bass is the largest string instrument in the orchestra – and it also reaches down to the lowest notes among the strings. Although not always the case, it is usually played with a bow in an orchestral setting. In the jazz world, it tends to be plucked and provides much the same role as a bass guitar does in a rock band. Usually relegated to the back of the orchestra, it does very occasionally get to be the star of the show. The Austrian composer Karl Ditters von Dittersdorf wrote no fewer than two concertos for the double bass.

† **Recommended Listening:**

The elephant from the *Carnival of the Animals*
by Saint-Saëns is played by the double bass.

DU PRÉ, JACQUELINE

1945-1987

Giving her first public performance at the age of seven, Jacqueline Du Pré made her debut at London's prestigious Wigmore Hall when she was just 16. As a performer, she was amazing to watch – player and instrument seem to meld together as one. She studied with the great cellists Mstislav Rostropovich and Paul Tortelier. Her recordings and performances of Elgar's *Cello Concerto* are regarded as being among the best ever and she became particularly closely linked with the work. She recorded it with her husband, Daniel Barenboim, conducting the Philadelphia Orchestra and with Sir John Barbirolli conducting the London Symphony Orchestra.

Sadly, Du Pré became ill with multiple sclerosis, gradually losing the feeling in her fingers and the ability to play. She died at the tragically young age of 42. The controversial 1998 film *Hilary and Jackie* is based on a book about her life, which was written by her brother and sister. The two cellos with which she became most associated – both made by Stradivarius – are now played by Yo-Yo Ma and by Nina Kotova.

Dvořák, Antonín
1841-1904

A great composer, Dvořak was a man who had interests in life aside from music. He was also a fanatical train spotter, a dedicated pigeon fancier and even had a passion for steamships. He spent his childhood helping in the family butcher's shop in a small Czech village. After studying music, he was a viola player in a Prague orchestra that was conducted by the great Czech composer Bedšich Smetana, before switching to concentrate his efforts on teaching and composing full-time.

Dvořák's music was undoubtedly nationalist in style and he remained very proud of his homeland, even though he travelled extensively. His music became popular in Britain and he made nine visits to the country, with some of his works receiving their premiere performances in cities such as Birmingham, London and Leeds.

In 1885, he took up a job in the USA as Director of the National Conservatoire of Music in New York. While he was in America, he became a great fan of African-American spirituals and used some of these melodies in his 'New World' Symphony, which remains his most widely recognised work today. The slow movement of this work became famous as the background music to the Hovis television adverts.

When he returned to Prague he mentored a new generation of Czech composers, including Suk and Novák.

† **Recommended Listening:**
  Song to the Moon from *Rusalka*

E

EARLY MUSIC

Early music is a group term for two, sometimes three, periods in music prior to the Classical period. Usually, it means the combined music of both the Medieval and Renaissance periods, although some definitions take in Baroque as being early, too. We don't think that is the case and treat the Baroque period as being a completely separate entity.

The Medieval and Renaissance periods together cover just about all music-making up until 1600, with the Medieval one ending at 1400. Although there was undoubtedly music-making before AD 500, this is the rough date from which many musical histories start. The Renaissance sub-period of Early music covers the two centuries between 1400 and 1600.

Aside from this date-based definition, Early music is sometimes used today as a term for music which has been rediscovered in our time, and for which authentic forms of performance are pursued. This is sometimes known as the 'Early Music Movement'.

Between 500 and 1400, the principal surviving music is plainchant. It had been handed down for centuries already by the year 500. A bishop called Ambrose gave his name to an early variety (known as Ambrosian chant). Many of the formal rules around plainchant were organised by Pope Gregory the Great, who lent his name to Gregorian chant – a sub-grouping of plainchant which has proved extremely popular in the late 20th and early 21st centuries. Pope Gregory was responsible for formalising chant through his Schola Cantorum, which was not just a papal choir but a whole system of handing down choir music from generation to generation. He also produced publications such as *The Antiphonar*, a compendium of chants.

As ancient and far removed as this period may seem to us now, it was a time of amazing and exciting developments. Worthy of mention is Guido d'Arrezzo, a Benedictine monk who died around 1050, but not before inventing what we now know as the musical stave – the five lines on which all music is written. Hildegaard of Bingen, who lived until 1179, was a significant composer, scholar, abbess and mystic. Her close links with the ruling class around Europe enabled her to take her own unique compositions onto an international stage. Hildegaard is considered part of what is now termed the *ars antiqua* (old art), a term generally applied to those working up to around the early 1300s.

This period of Early music also included the delightful round, *Sumer is icumen in*, often attributed to the Norfolk-born John of Fornsete. Worthy of mention, too, is Franco of Cologne, a German composer of the mid-1200s, who standardised the measure of notes by codifying the lengths and appearance of minims, breves, crotchets, and so on.

After 1300, the *ars antiqua* was replaced by the *ars nova*, when plainchant gave way to polyphony. This is where a composer writes separate tunes for people with different voices (sopranos, tenors, basses and so on), which all combine together harmoniously. Among the principle composers of the *ars nova* was the Frenchman Guillaume de Machaut, who is credited with being a driving force in the development of musical polyphony.

The Renaissance in music, from 1400 to 1600, saw a rapid rebirth of styles and ideas about how music should be composed. It was the immediate precursor to Baroque period, and the most celebrated composers of the time include:

Josquin des Prez (1450s–1521): prolific Franco-Flemish composer. His mass, *La Sol Fa Re Mi* is said to be based on the phrase, *Laise faire moy* (Leave it to me).

John Taverner (1490–1545): the most important English composer of the time, writing masses (such as his important *Western Wind Mass*) out of Oxford. Not to be confused with the contemporary composer Sir John Tavener.

Giovanni Pierluigi da Palestrina (1525–1594): Chief exponent of the Roman School of the Renaissance, a largely geographical group of choral writers, which extended into the Baroque period and later included Allegri.

EINAUDI, LUDOVICO
1955-

Born in Turin in 1955, Einaudi studied piano and composition first at the Milan Conservatoire and then with the highly-regarded contemporary Italian composer, Luciano Berio. He came to prominence in Britain in the mid-1990s with his solo piano album, *Le Onde*. Although he has written for film and for full orchestra, his other solo piano albums *I Giorni* and *Una Mattina* have become more enduringly popular. His compositions embrace the sparse, repetitive style of many of the minimalist composers and his music has great ambient and contemplative qualities.

† **Recommended Listening:**
  Duo Tramonti from the album *Eden Roc*

ELGAR, EDWARD
1857-1934

Acknowledged by many as being England's greatest-ever composer, Edward Elgar was born into a musical family. His father ran a music shop in Worcester and was also the local travelling piano tuner. One of Elgar's earliest memories was of journeying around with his father on a horse and cart to tune pianos in smart country houses across Worcestershire. Although he learned piano, violin and organ as a youngster, he tried to 'do the right thing' by working in a solicitor's office. He hated it, though, and, by the time he was 16, he was working as a freelance musician. Elgar did not enjoy expensive private musical tuition, nor did he study at a top-rated *conservatoire*. Much of what he learned, he taught himself.

By the turn of the 20th century, Elgar was composing extensively, fulfilling a particular need from English festivals and music societies for big choral works. He already had *The Black Knight*, *King Olaf* and *The Light of Life* under his belt. He was still teaching violin to pay the bills, but he had enormous success in London with the premiere of his *Variations on an Original Theme* (now known as the *Enigma Variations*).

In 1900, he wrote *The Dream of Gerontius*, another choral barnstormer, which was premiered at the Birmingham Festival under the baton of the German conductor Hans Richter, one of the composer's early champions. It helped to get him noticed in Germany, where Richard Strauss described him as being the leading English composer of the day.

This was Elgar's most creative period, with respect for his music growing with each new composition. Two symphonies, his *Violin Concerto*, the oratorios *The Apostles* and *The Kingdom* and his *Introduction for Allegro and Strings* all came in quick succession, to great acclaim. Not for him the premiere of a new work which then lay forgotten in the bottom drawer of his desk – his *Symphony No. 1* was performed an incredible 100 times in cities right across Europe.

When the words by A.C. Benson were put to a section of his *Pomp and Circumstance March No. 1*, it was clear that Elgar had a runaway hit on his hands – so much so, that *Land of Hope and Glory* sits alongside *Jerusalem* as an unofficial national anthem. Today, we are still able to hear many of Elgar's works exactly as he wanted them to be played because of his passion for the newly invented gramophone recording. Listening to the recorded results of these early sessions now may not exactly be hi-fi, but it does give us a huge insight into Elgar's music.

Elgar was knighted in 1904 and became Master of the King's Music in 1924. He spent his last years back home in Worcestershire.

† Recommended Listening:

Cello Concerto
Violin Concerto
Pomp and Circumstance March No. 1
Cockaigne Overture
Introduction and Allegro for Strings
The Dream of Gerontius

ENIGMA VARIATIONS

First performed in London in 1899, this piece has fostered more debate than almost any other British classical music work. It is dedicated to a group of Elgar's friends, each of whom is represented by the musical characteristics in each of the 14 individual movements. There was, however, an added mystery. Elgar suggested that there was an 'enigma' hidden in the piece, possibly a second well-known tune. Nobody has ever satisfactorily unlocked the code, although many people have spent a lot of time trying. Elgar took the secret of the enigma with him to his grave.

ENCORE

The French word for 'again' is shouted by audiences at the end of a concert to encourage the performers to play a little bit more. It is also the name for the pieces themselves that are played at the end of the concert, which are often designed to show off a performer's talents at the very best. Some performers become as famous for their encores as they are for playing the main body of their concerts. Although they are made to look spontaneous, most encores are prepared in advance. An interesting footnote: although 'encore' is a French word, it is not what concertgoers in France shout when they want more from a performer. Perplexingly, the French for encore is *bis*, which translates into English as twice.

F

FALLA, MANUEL DE
1876-1946

This Spanish composer spent his twenties studying piano and composition and only started to receive recognition for his music when he had almost turned 30. He moved to Paris in 1907 and became friends with the French composers Debussy, Ravel and Dukas. He also met the Russian composer Stravinsky and the impresario Diaghilev. After the First World War, he went back to Spain. Diaghilev commissioned de Falla to write the score for the ballet *The Three Cornered Hat*, which had its premiere at the Alhambra Theatre in London's Leicester Square, next door to where Classic FM's studios are now based. Becoming disillusioned with his homeland because of the Spanish Civil War, he spent the last seven years of his life in Argentina.

† **Recommended Listening:**
    The Ritual Fire Dance from the ballet *El amor brujo*

FAURÉ, GABRIEL
1845-1924

A whizz on the organ and a great composer in his own right, Fauré was also responsible for passing on his expertise to a whole new generation of French composers during the 15-year period that he was Director of the Paris Conservatoire. He himself studied with Saint-Saëns, and his pupils included Maurice Ravel and Nadia Boulanger; the latter was responsible for giving his *Requiem* a wider hearing.

Fauré had written it to be performed at his local church and, despite Boulanger's best efforts, it still took until after the end of the Second World War before it was widely recognised as being the masterpiece that it surely is. It also took him quite a while to get noticed outside of France. Towards the end of his life he became deaf. It didn't stop him from giving composition advice right to the end – not least to *Les Six*, the group of young French composers which included Satie and Poulenc.

† **Recommended Listening:**
  Pavane

FIELD, JOHN
1782-1837
Field was already wowing the crowds in his home city of Dublin by the time he was ten years old. So much so, that his father took him off to London to seek his fame and fortune. There, he studied with the piano genius Muzio Clementi and just got better and better. Field always saw himself as a pianist who composed, rather than purely as a composer. He travelled around Europe playing Clementi's compositions, ultimately settling in St. Petersburg. He developed a series of 20 short pieces for the piano, which he called *Nocturnes*. The idea was taken on and developed by Chopin, who became famous for them, but it was actually Field who invented them in the first place.

† **Recommended Listening:**
  Piano Concerto No. 2

FILM MUSIC
There are two types of classical music used in films: the first is where a film director borrows an existing classical work and uses it to complement

the pictures and the second happens when a brand new music score is commissioned especially for the movie.

Some of the most famous examples of the former include Rachmaninov's *Piano Concerto No. 2*, which features in *Brief Encounter*; Mozart's *Clarinet Concerto* in *Out of Africa*; Richard Strauss's *Also Sprach Zarathustra* in *2001: A Space Odyssey*; and even Mozart's *Eine Kleine Nachtmusik* in the unlikely setting of *Ace Ventura: Pet Detective*.

In *Fantasia*, Walt Disney created a whole animated film with a score provided by the classical greats, including Bach, Beethoven, Dukas, Ponchielli, Mussorgsky, Tchaikovsky, Schubert and Stravinsky. There was even a live action role for the Philadelphia Orchestra and their conductor Leopold Stokowski. Upon seeing the section featuring the *Pastoral Symphony*, Walt Disney is reported to have said: 'Gee! That'll make Beethoven!'

The very first film soundtrack ever written was composed by Saint-Saëns for the 1908 movie *L'Assassinat du Duc de Guise*. Since then, a whole list of mainstream classical composers have written specifically for the silver screen, including Arnold, Britten, Copland, Glass, Khachaturian, Korngold, Prokofiev, Shostakovich, Vaughan Williams and Walton. The link between film soundtracks and core classical music is irrefutable – in many ways, it is a natural development of the long tradition of composers writing incidental music to accompany stage plays.

This list of those composers who have made their names writing specifically for the big screen is an A to Z all of its own:

Richard Addinsell penned the *Warsaw Concerto* as a pastiche of a Romantic piano concerto for the 1941 film *Dangerous Moonlight*, as well as the scores for *Goodbye Mr. Chips* and *The Prince and the Showgirl*. The Italian Ennio Morricone began his professional life playing in a jazz band, but ended up scoring films ranging from *The Mission* to *The Good, The Bad & The Ugly*. Yorkshire-born John Barry inherited his love of films from his father, who was a cinema projectionist. His big hits include *Dances with Wolves*, *Born Free* and *Out of Africa*. He is of the same generation as the undoubted king of the living film composers, John Williams, who has enjoyed a partnership with the director Stephen Spielberg that has spanned decades. Williams, who writes using a pencil and manuscript paper in a small office on a Los Angeles film lot, created the scores for hits such as *ET*, *Star Wars*, *Schindler's List* and *Superman*.

Elmer Bernstein was one of the heavyweights of the soundtrack world, penning such delights as the music to *The Magnificent Seven*, while Max Steiner wrote the theme for *Gone With the Wind*. And then there was Eric Coates, who gave us *The Dambusters march* – a work that, in fact, he had already written before the film came along. He just needed somewhere to put it. Jerry Goldsmith was another of the giants of the film music world, his scores range from *Star Trek* to *The Omen*. In terms of scary soundtracks, it would be impossible to miss out Bernard Herrmann and the music to *Psycho* from any comprehensive list.

Craig Armstrong (*Romeo and Juliet*) and Patrick Doyle (*Sense and Sensibility*) are among Scotland's most successful film composers. England offers Howard Goodall (*Mr Bean*), Nigel Hess (*Ladies in Lavender*), Rachel Portman (*Chocolat*), Stephen Warbeck (*Shakespeare in Love*) and Debbie Wiseman (*Wilde*). Two other current big names are the USA's James Horner (*Titanic* and *Braveheart*) and Canada's Howard Shore (*The Lord of the Rings*).

Klaus Badelt is one of a new generation of film composers, working for Hans Zimmer's 'movie music factory' at one stage, with his theme for *Pirates of the Caribbean* being especially well-known to current movie goers. Zimmer himself is the man behind the music for *Gladiator*.

Finzi, Gerald
1901-1956

One of the most underrated English composers, Finzi deserves to be mentioned in the same breath as Elgar and Vaughan Williams. His settings of the poems of Thomas Hardy are particularly beautiful. He did a lot to revive the music of older and lesser-known English composers, such as William Boyce and John Stanley, with performances of their works being given by his group, the Newbury String Players. Two interesting footnotes: between 1941 and 1945, he worked in the Ministry of War Transport; he also became an expert cultivator of rare apples.

† **Recommended Listening:**
Eclogue

FLUTE

Flutes go back to ancient Egyptian times and beyond. Variants of the instrument are also present in areas of world music, but here we are concentrating on flutes used in the Western classical music tradition.

Despite being part of the woodwind family, the flute is now rarely made of wood, instead being manufactured from metal. The instrument was originally known as the 'Transverse flute' or the 'German flute'. It was given the first name because it is designed to be played sideways, unlike, say, a recorder (which was sometimes known as the 'English flute'). The 'German' epithet came about because the instrument seems to have hailed from that country in the distant past.

Flutes are distinct from all other woodwind instruments because they have no reed. The player simply blows into the metal tube and creates the notes via the finger-holes positioned along the length of the instrument. The flute's range runs three octaves up from Middle C – that's a range of 24 notes, hitting the high notes with ease.

Famous flautists (the correct name for a flute player) include James Galway, who was a massive hit in the 1970s and 1980s as 'the man with the golden flute', and Emmanuel Pahud, the principal flautist of the Berlin Philharmonic Orchestra.

† **Recommended Listening:**
Debussy's *Syrinx*

FRANCK, CÉSAR
1822-1890
One of Belgium's greatest classical music exports, Franck was touring by the age of 11 and moved with his family to Paris to study at the Conservatoire there until relatively late on his life. His music failed to capture the imagination of the French public. He worked as an organist and rose to fame for his playing – and particularly for his improvisations. At the age of 50, he became a Professor at the Conservatoire. Gradually, his works were performed more and more. His pleasant demeanour and general good nature led to him being nicknamed 'Pére Franck' by those who knew him.
† **Recommended Listening:**
  Panis Angelicus

FRENCH HORN
Uncoil the French horn and you would have eleven feet of brass piping on your hands. Originating from the world of hunting, the horn started to make an appearance in the world of orchestral music in France around the time of Jean-Baptiste Lully. Valves were added in 1827 and composers such as Schumann and Wagner were big fans of this more modern instrument. The effect of the valves was to make it an easier instrument to play as the performers did not have to create all of the different notes themselves. Modern French horns are made in five parts: the main body, the mouthpiece, the 'bell' (the round part the player sticks his or her hand up), the mouth pipe and the valves. French horns make a wonderful sound: when they are played softly, they can sound pastoral and placid; and when they are loud, they can be menacing and regal.
† **Recommended Listening:**
  Mozart's Horn Concerto No. 4

G

GERSHWIN, GEORGE
1898-1937

Born and brought up in New York, Gershwin was the son of Russian Jewish migrants. He was brought up on classical music, but his own personal tastes ran far wider. After leaving school, at the age of 15, he worked as a song-plugger on what was then known as 'Tin Pan Alley'.

Gershwin was soon plugging his own songs, with *Swanee* his first big hit in 1920. In fact, he made so much money from this one song over the years that it allowed him to spend his time writing just about anything else he liked.

In 1924, he wrote *Rhapsody in Blue*, a wonderful fusion of jazz and classical music. By now, he was a multimillionaire, living in a swanky house on New York's Upper West Side. As well as his other big classical hits, such as *An American in Paris* and his *Piano Concerto in F*, he also wrote his massively popular opera, *Porgy and Bess*, featuring the song *Summertime*.

Gershwin died at the tragically young age of 38 from a brain tumour. He continued to take lessons on writing for orchestra well into his thirties and it seems certain that, had he lived, he could well have gone on to become an even greater success as a classical composer. His music remains hugely popular on both sides of the Atlantic today, not least because the knack of being able to pen an infectiously catchy tune, which he learned on Tin Pan Alley, never left him.

† **Recommended Listening:**
Rhapsody in Blue

GIBBONS, ORLANDO
1583-1625

Gibbons moved in exalted 17th century circles: born in Oxford, he sang in the choir of King's College, Cambridge, and studied music at the university. The organist at both the Chapel Royal and Westminster Abbey, he also worked as one of the King's chamber musicians. He died in Canterbury after suffering an apoplectic fit and was buried in the Cathedral there. During his relatively short life, he wrote some notable church anthems, including *This is the Record of John*.

GLASS, PHILIP
1937-

This American composer has an unconventional classical music background, having studied with both the legendary French teacher Nadia Boulanger and the Indian sitar virtuoso Ravi Shankar. In 1967, he formed the Philip Glass Ensemble and writing for this group of seven musicians formed the core of his output for many years. The style of music that he developed was dubbed 'minimalism'. It is distinctive, catchy and mesmerising and Glass has sustained his popularity ever since, both as a composer of core classical works and of film soundtracks.

† **Recommended Listening:**
  Violin Concerto

GLAZUNOV, ALEXANDER
1865-1936

Born in St. Petersburg, Glazunov had lessons from Rimsky-Korsakov, who said that he progressed 'not by the day, but literally by the hour'. He was lucky enough to find a rich sponsor in Mitrofan Belyayev early on, so a lot of his music was published and paid for without any of the struggles that other composers had to endure. Belyayev introduced him to Liszt, who became an influence on the young composer. Glazunov's music is on the conservative side, but that does not mean that it is not beautiful – his *Saxophone Concerto* of 1931 is particularly stunning. As an instrumentalist, he was something of a polymath, learning to play the piano, violin, cello, trumpet, French horn, clarinet and a range of percussion instruments.

† **Recommended Listening:**

The Seasons

GLINKA, MIKHAIL

1804-1857

Glinka's parents were fairly wealthy, allowing him the creative freedom to do what he wanted without fear of ever suffering poverty. He studied for a short period with the Irish composer John Field, before travelling to Italy, where he developed a love of opera. His first smash hit was *A Life for the Tsar* and it propelled him to the position of being the first great Russian opera composer. His music virtually defined the Russian Nationalist sound overnight. Glinka's second opera, *Russlan and Ludmilla* cemented his success outside his homeland. He created unquestionably Russian music for the rest of his life, paving the way for a new generation of great Russian composers, all of whom continued to write music that relied heavily on their native folk sounds for its inspiration.

† **Recommended Listening:**

Overture to *Russlan and Ludmilla*

GLUCK, CHRISTOPH WILLIBALD VON

1714-1787

This German cellist and composer was lucky enough to spend his formative years fairly loaded down with princely patrons, who paid his way. He studied in Milan and developed a penchant for opera, becoming much in demand as a composer. By the 1750s, he started to develop the idea of enhancing the drama in operas, as well as the singing. The reform did not always go down well with the divas on the stage, but it was a huge step forward in the history of opera and set a new benchmark for the composers who followed him. He made plenty of cash along the way and was to be found living in quite some style in Vienna at the end of his life. He died after quaffing an after dinner liqueur – against his doctor's orders.

† **Recommended Listening:**
Dance of the Blessed Spirits from the opera *Orpheus and Euridice*

GOODALL, HOWARD
1958-

Among the most successful film and television theme tune writers of all time, Goodall's credits include *Blackadder*, *Mr Bean*, *Red Dwarf*, *The Catherine Tate Show*, *QI* and *The Vicar of Dibley*. He is well-known for his choral music and as Classic FM's third Composer in Residence, he wrote *Enchanted Voices*, an album based on the Beatitudes, which stormed to the top of the Specialist Classical Charts upon its release and stayed there for months, winning a Classic FM Gramophone Award in the process. He was named Composer of the Year at the Classical Brit Awards in 2009, following the release of *Eternal Light: A Requiem*, which was incorporated into a ballet by the Ballet Rambert. As well as presenting a weekly programme on Classic FM, he has become a regular face on television, presenting award-winning series such as *Howard Goodall's Big Bangs* for Channel 4. Goodall is also a passionate advocate of the benefits of music education and is England's first National Singing Ambassador.

† **Recommended Listening:**
Enchanted Voices

GÓRECKI, HENRYK
1933-

Originally a primary school teacher, Górecki switched to studying music and started to make a name after his *Beatus Vir* was performed during Pope John Paul II's visit to Poland in 1979. His writing was influenced by avant-garde composers such as Stockhausen but, in the end, he became known for composing chants with simple, rich harmonies. His success in the UK will forever be tied to the launch of Classic FM, with his *Symphony No. 3* (subtitled *A Symphony of Sorrowful Songs*) becoming a sensational hit during the station's first year of existence, despite the fact that it had actually been composed and received its premiere some 15 years earlier.

† **Recommended Listening:**

  Symphony No. 3

GOUNOD, CHARLES
1818-1893

When he was 21 years old, Gounod won the Prix de Rome composition prize and went on to become an organist in Paris – a pathway followed by many of the great French composers. In his thirties, he began to write operas, but success only came in his forties with Faust. He spent a good deal of time in England and his oratorio *Mors et Vita,* one particular part of which has become something of a hit among Classic FM listeners, was premiered at the Birmingham Festival. He is known to many nowadays for his addition to Bach's *Prelude No. 1* of an overlaying tune, which is now usually referred to as Gounod's *Ave Maria*.

† **Recommended Listening:**

  Judex from *Mors et Vita*

GRAINGER, PERCY
1882-1961

Grainger challenges Erik Satie for the title of 'most eccentric composer' in our A to Z. Australian born, he married his 'Nordic Princess' Ella Viola Ström in front of thousands at the Hollywood Bowl. He was nicknamed 'the Jogging Pianist' because he used to run to piano concerts and rush up on stage at the last minute. Not only did he make his own clothes, but he also designed early prototypes of the woman's sports bra. A good friend of Grieg and Delius, he was a great collector of folk tunes. He spent the latter part of his life inventing complicated musical formats using early electronic instruments.

† **Recommended Listening:**

Music for an English Country Garden

GRANADOS, ENRIQUE
1867-1916

After studying in Paris and Barcelona, Granados went on to found his own concert season and piano school in the Spanish city. In his day, he was a pianist first and a composer second. He was especially highly regarded as a performer of his own piano works. His music is unquestionably Spanish in style and this has ensured his enduring popularity in his homeland. Granados and his wife were both drowned when the *Sussex*, the boat which they were travelling upon from Liverpool to Dieppe, was torpedoed by a German submarine. Classical music was robbed of a talent who would have continued on to even greater things.

† **Recommended Listening:**

Spanish Dance No. 5

GRIEG, EDVARD
1843-1907

Norway's finest composer was born in 1843, the same year that the first commercial Christmas card was commissioned and dispatched. Although always considered Norwegian, Grieg's great-grandfather was Scottish. As a youngster, Grieg showed great flair for the piano and he was sent to Leipzig to study music. Despite not particularly enjoying himself there, Grieg honed his musical genius in the city. He started to build himself up quite a celebrity fan club, with Liszt, Delius and Grainger all fully paid up members. He was also good friends with the playwright Henrik Ibsen, who asked him to write the incidental music to his play *Peer Gynt*. Grieg became a huge star in Norway and something of a national treasure. In his later life, he became famous as a travelling concert pianist, performing his *Piano Concerto* in cities across Europe. Grieg is buried half way up the side of a rock face, near Troldhaugen. Apparently, the composer was out walking one evening and noticed how the sun hit a spot, half way up the mountain side. He told a friend who was with him: 'There... I would like to rest for ever!'

† **Recommended Listening:**

Piano Concerto

GUIDO D'AREZZO
c.955 – c.1050

One of the oldest personalities in our A to Z, we have a lot to thank this Italian monk for. He invented a system called 'solmisation', which he used to help other monks learn chants very quickly. By giving names to musical notes, people could work out where they were on the scale – it was the same principle used by Julie Andrews to teach the von Trapp children in *The Sound of Music*. Guido wrote about it in *Micrologus*, which was published around the year 1025, earning him widespread fame across Italy. Today, he is widely regarded as the father of modern musical notation.

GUITAR

Although the guitar is a stringed instrument and a classical music instrument at that, it is not usually considered as being a stringed instrument in the orchestral sense – mainly because, unlike the violin, viola, cello and double bass, it is never played with a bow. The guitar that we know today is actually a member of the lute family. It has six strings, which are tuned to E, A, D, G, B and E. The back and sides of a good classical guitar are usually made of Brazilian rosewood; the neck is cedar; the fingerboard is ebony; and the face is spruce. Over the years composers such as Boccherini, Berlioz and Paganini composed for the instrument. Probably the greatest guitar work of all was composed by the Spaniard Joaquín Rodrigo – the *Concierto de Aranjuez*. It became a staple part of the repertoire for two great guitar virtuosos in the latter part of the 20th century: the Englishman Julian Bream and the Australian John Williams.

† **Recommended Listening:**

Tárrega's *Recuerdos de la Alhambra*

H

HALLÉ ORCHESTRA

Founded in Manchester in 1858 by the respected pianist and conductor, Charles Hallé, the Hallé Orchestra is the UK's second oldest continuously operating professional symphony orchestra, only beaten to the title of being the oldest by near neighbours, the Royal Liverpool Philharmonic, which can trace its origin as a professional band back to 1853. The Hallé's home venue is the wonderful Bridgewater Hall in the centre of Manchester and the orchestra has a long association with the cities of Sheffield and Bradford. The orchestra is currently enjoying an artistic resurgence under Music Director, Sir Mark Elder. He follows in a long line of prestigious Principal Conductors, including Hans Richter, Sir Thomas Beecham, Sir Hamilton Harty and Sir John Barbirolli. The orchestra's list of world premiere performances includes Elgar's *Symphony No. 1*, Vaughan Williams' *Sinfonia Antartica* and Finzi's *Cello Concerto*.

HANDEL, GEORGE FRIDERIC
1685-1759

Born in the German town of Halle, Handel was the son of a barber-surgeon, who was firmly against his boy following a career in music. Instead, Handel was encouraged to study law at Halle University and was only able to follow his musical dream once his father had died. He had always kept up his music and was well-known among the local musicians. By 1702, he was composing and playing the organ in Halle Cathedral. He had also met the prolific Baroque composer Telemann.

In 1703, he travelled to Hamburg, where he played violin in the opera house orchestra. He also started to compose operas. There was nowhere better to perfect this craft than Italy and so he packed his bags once again. Once in Italy, he became friendly with Corelli and both Domenico and Alessandro Scarlatti. His opera *Agrippina* was immensely popular and he ended up working as Court Conductor to the Elector of Hanover. Despite the steady income that this gave him, Handel hankered for something more and was granted an extended sabbatical to allow him to ply his operatic trade in London.

Once again, his operas proved to be enormously successful: *Rinaldo*, which he wrote in just 15 days, was given its premiere at the Haymarket Theatre and turned him into an overnight sensation. Handel began to move in royal circles, though there was a short period of difficulty for him when the Elector of Hanover, from whose court he had been absent for far longer than expected, came to the English throne as George I. All was quickly forgiven and forgotten, though, following the success of his opera *Amadigi*. In fact, he ended up receiving a pension for life from the crown. He composed his enduringly popular *Water Music* for George I and wrote his anthem *Zadok the Priest* for the coronation of George II. It has been sung at every coronation since.

The operas kept coming and Handel also produced a series of oratorios, including *Messiah* and *Solomon*. A naturalised Englishman, his place in the country's musical history was by now assured. No major event was complete without one of his works, such as the *Music for the Royal Fireworks*, which he wrote as part of the celebrations to mark the signing of the Aix-la-Chapelle peace treaty in 1748.

When he died in 1759, Handel was a national figure and was buried in Westminster Abbey. His music continued to dominate his adopted homeland for at least the next century and, alongside Johann Sebastian Bach, he remains the most significant of all of the composers of the Baroque period.

There were some striking coincidences that link Handel and J.S. Bach together: both were born in the same year; both suffered from cataracts; and both were blinded by botched treatment from the same English surgeon.

† **Recommended Listening:**

Music for the Royal Fireworks
Water Music
Zadok the Priest
Ombra Mai Fu from *Xerxes*
Arrival of the Queen of Sheba from *the oratorio Solomon*

MESSIAH

Premiered in Dublin in 1742, this is Handel's greatest oratorio, beloved of choral societies the world over. In some ways, it is odd that Handel is most remembered for a religious work, as he spent far more time composing secular operas than church music. The libretto was put together from the Bible by Handel's friend, Charles Jennens and the music took Handel just three weeks to compose. The *Hallelujah Chorus* is a wonderfully life-affirming highlight of the work. It is worth noting that this work's correct title does not include the definitive article.

Harmony

The best way of explaining harmony in music is to borrow some thinking from the world of mathematics. Taking the x and y axis, one is vertical and the other horizontal. Music works in much the same way. If we take one note and keep playing it, we are hearing it 'horizontally', so to speak. Putting other notes next to it allows a tune, or melody to give it its correct name, to proceed horizontally. But, if we take that original note and simultaneously add other notes above and below it, then we have a chord. More than one note, voiced vertically on our axis is harmony.

HARP

This is an instrument that has been in existence since ancient times and has developed in many different shapes and sizes over the years. The modern concert harp usually has 46 or 47 strings, which gives it a range of six-and-half octaves. That is not quite as much as a piano, but is still pretty wide-ranging: it means that a harp can play notes as deep as a double bass and as high as a piccolo. Harps also have pedals, which the harpists press once to raise the string up one note and then press again to raise it up another note. The need for simultaneous hand and foot co-ordination makes it an incredibly hard instrument to play, while keeping a harp in tune is almost a full-time job in itself. The Prince of Wales has recently re-established the position of court harpist. The first holder of the title was Catrin Finch; the current court harpist is Claire Jones.

† **Recommended Listening:**

Mozart's *Flute and Harp Concerto*

HARPSICHORD

This small keyboard was the forerunner to the piano. The main difference between the two instruments is that the harpsichord does not hammer the strings inside its casing as a piano does. Instead, it plucks them with a pin. The inner workings of a harpsichord contain a series of around 48 strings, each with its own pin plucker and a spruce or cedar soundboard, which helps to amplify the sound. Although harpsichords are still played today, the invention of the piano has rendered them far less popular than they were in Baroque times and they remain an instrument that listeners tend either to love or to hate.

† **Recommended Listening:**

C.P.E. Bach's *Harpsichord Concerto in D minor*

HAWES, PATRICK
1958-

Patrick Hawes is one of a long line of English composers who have drawn their inspiration from their native countryside. His music sits comfortably within the English Romantic tradition of Delius and Vaughan Williams. Classic FM's second composer in residence, between 2006 and 2007, he is also a highly proficient organist. Hawes first came to widespread notice with his haunting vocal work *Quanta Qualia*, taken from his album *Blue in Blue*. It entered the annual listeners' poll, the Classic FM Hall of Fame, shortly after its release on CD, making it the fastest ever new entry for a new composer on the chart. Other major works include *Song of Songs*, *Fair Albion*; *Visions of England* and the *Lazarus Requiem*, premiered at the Cadogen Hall, London, in April 2008.

† **Recommended Listening:**

   Towards the Light, an album of reflective piano works.

HAYDN, JOSEPH
1732-1809

Born in the year that London's first Royal Opera House opened for business, Haydn was one of the big names of the Classical period of classical music. By the time he was just five years old, he was showing amazing musical talent. Three years later, he became a choirboy at St. Stephen's Cathedral in Venice. During this period, it was suggested to him that he might like to consider becoming a castrato, but once the surgical operation needed to achieve this was explained to him, he declined the offer. When his voice did break, Haydn worked as a teacher and accompanist. It was a pretty lean period in financial terms and Haydn struggled, at first, before picking up commissions for new works from aristocratic patrons.

At the age of 29, his life changed when he was given a job by Prince Paul Esterházy. He remained in the service of the Esterházy family for the next three decades. Prince Paul's successor, Prince Nikolaus, built a secluded palace, which was modelled on Versailles. It meant that Haydn could compose without anyone to distract him, with the exception of his wife. She did not appreciate his music and he did not appreciate much about her at all.

Haydn was a prolific composer and his name is particularly associated with the symphony. In total, he wrote 104 catalogued symphonies and, in doing so, changed the direction of the genre completely. He gained the nickname 'Papa Haydn' because he came to be regarded as the 'father' of the symphony.

Haydn's fame spread when he was in his forties and fifties. Just before he was 60, Prince Nikolaus died. Even though the Esterházy family then ceased to employ any musicians, Haydn continued to be paid. He took the opportunity to travel to England, Spain and France and bought a house for himself in Vienna. During this period, he took on pupils, such as Ludwig van Beethoven, who was just a teenage boy. Wherever he went, his visits were treated as major musical events, with other composers, members of royal families and academics falling over themselves to pay their respects. His music was both critically acclaimed and financially highly lucrative.

In 1796, the Esterházy family reintroduced music-making at their court and Haydn was back in his old job, although he was only required to write music for special occasions. During this period, he composed the oratorios *The Creation* and *The Seasons*.

It is true to say that Haydn may not have led the most adventurous or exciting life, but his relatively comfortable circumstances allowed him the time and space to compose many masterpieces. Musically, he was a real innovator. He died shortly after his 77th birthday – a grand old age for the time.

SYMPHONIES

Haydn wrote his first symphony in 1757 and his last in 1795. The first 30 followed the old-fashioned Italian style, with three movements, the first and last of which were fast, with a slow section sandwiched in the middle. From *Symphony No. 31* onwards, all of his symphonies are in four movements (usually fast/slow/fast/fast).

Many of them were given nicknames:

Symphony No. 22 The Philosopher
Symphony No. 55 The Schoolmaster
Symphony No. 60 The Distraught Man
Symphony No. 82 The Bear
Symphony No. 83 The Hen
Symphony No. 94 Surprise
Symphony No. 100 Military
Symphony No. 101 Clock
Symphony No. 103 Drumroll
Symphony No. 104 London

HILDEGARD OF BINGEN
1098-1179

It is hard not to come to the conclusion that classical music is primarily a man's world. Certainly, the number of successful composers over the years is weighted heavily in the favour of men. However, one of the earliest composers to feature in our A to Z is, in fact, a woman. Hildegard lived for 81 years, during which time she founded nunneries and wrote major theological works, plays and music. She was also an expert on politics, poetry and medicine. One of the most prominent individuals of her day, she corresponded with many other leading figures. Musically, she was a mistress of plainchant, writing pieces to honour the saints and the Virgin Mary.

† **Recommended Listening:**
Ordo Virtutum

HOLST, GUSTAV
1874-1934

While he was studying at the Royal College of Music, Holst began a lifelong friendship with his contemporary Vaughan Williams. During the holidays, Holst played trombone in a seaside band and after leaving the college he played professionally as a trombonist for the Scottish Orchestra (now the Royal Scottish National Orchestra). In 1903, he began working as a music teacher at Dulwich Girls' School, a post he combined with being Director of Music at St. Paul's Girls' School from 1905 and Director of Music at Morley College from 1907. In 1919, he was made Professor of Music at the University of Reading and also worked as a professor at his alma mater. Holst's first major success was *The Planets*, an impressive orchestral suite; it remains his best-known work. Aside from composing, he was a keen cyclist – even going on a biking holiday to Algiers.

† **Recommended Listening:**

Jupiter from *The Planets*

I

Incidental Music

Most of the incidental music that is composed today is commissioned for cinema or television, as soundtracks alongside films or TV dramas. This was not always the case. Long before movies came along, most major composers from the 1800s onwards had the odd commission for incidental music under their belts, so it is important to draw a distinction between what is and what is not classed as incidental music. Although operas, operettas and even sometimes oratorios are written to be performed as staged works, the music for these is not thought of as being 'incidental' – instead, it is part of the main event, if you like. On the other hand, music written either to accompany dialogue in a play, or to fill in between scenes (such as 'entr'actes' and 'interludes'), very firmly does fall in the incidental music camp. Two famous examples are the music written by Mendelssohn for Shakespeare's *A Midsummer Night's Dream* and by Grieg for Ibsen's *Peer Gynt*.

Intermezzo

By a quirk of the alphabet, incidental music and intermezzo appear next to each other and the latter is a good example of the former. Literally translated as 'in the middle', an intermezzo was originally a short opera, often featuring comic characters, that was performed between the acts of a more serious opera. By the 19th century, however, the meaning of intermezzo had changed to being a piece of orchestral music that denoted the passage of time. Two good examples are the intermezzo from Mascagni's opera *Cavalleria Rusticana* and *The Walk to the Paradise Garden* from Delius's opera *A Village Romeo and Juliet*.

J

JANÁČEK, LEOŠ
1854-1928

This Czech composer was virtually unknown outside his homeland for most of his life. He worked as a composer, conductor, organist and teacher. His masterpiece is the opera *Jenufa*, which was first performed when he was 50 years old. It was a success in Brno, where it was debuted, but, because Janášek had fallen out with the head of the Prague Opera, it took another 12 years for the work to reach the Czech capital. When it was finally performed there, the opera was incredibly warmly received, with the result that Janác̆ek, now aged 62, became an overnight success. This spurred him on to compose other acclaimed works, such as *The Cunning Little Vixen*, another opera, and his *Glagolitic Mass*. The conductor Sir Charles Mackerras has been a leading champion of his music.

† **Recommended Listening:**
  Sinfonietta

JENKINS, KARL
1944-

Wales's most successful living classical composer hails from Swansea. He studied at the University of Wales and at the Royal Academy of Music in London. Initially, he played oboe in a ground-breaking jazz group called Nucleus, winning the 1970 Montreux Jazz Festival Prize. Next he joined the 'prog rock' band Soft Machine, which was a mainstay of the 'Canterbury Sound' of the 1970s. Eventually, composing took over and he enjoyed a highly successful career writing music for television commercials. Jenkins expanded many of these tunes into full-blown classical works and is today a popular and much sought-after composer. In 2000, he premiered *The Armed Man: A Mass for Peace*; his *Requiem* was first performed in 2005 and his *Stabat Mater* in 2008. His ear for a tune is second to none and he has proven time and time again that he has the ability to write modern classical music that strikes a chord with 21st century listeners.

† **Recommended Listening:**

Palladio

K

KENNEDY, NIGEL
1956-

One of the most recognisable classical music performers alive today, Nigel Kennedy was born into a musical family in Brighton. He studied piano with his mother, before going to the Yehudi Menuhin School in Surrey at the age of seven. He also studied in New York at the Julliard School. It emerged recently that Menuhin himself paid the youngster's school fees throughout his childhood. Alongside Menuhin, Kennedy's other great influence was the jazz violin player Stephane Grapelli.

Kennedy made his debut with the Berlin Philharmonic Orchestra at 24 and immediately became the talk of the musical world. His recording of *Elgar's Violin Concerto* was voted record of the year at the 1985 *Gramophone* Awards, setting him on the road to repeated success in the recording studio, with best-selling concerto recordings of Bach, Beethoven, Berg, Brahms, Bruch, Mendelssohn, Sibelius, Tchaikovsky and Walton, alongside chamber music and recital discs. His version of Vivaldi's *Four Seasons*, recorded with the English Chamber Orchestra in 1989, shot him into the big time, with sales of over 2 million worldwide.

Kennedy remains passionate about jazz and is as at home performing at Ronnie Scott's jazz club in London's Soho, as he is on the stage of a major European concert hall. He is also a devoted follower of Aston Villa football club, and has often been photographed wearing the team scarf while playing his violin. He is Artistic Director of the Polish Chamber Orchestra and divides his time between homes in London and Kraków.

† **Recommended Listening:**
Vivaldi's *Four Seasons*

KHACHATURIAN, ARAM
1903-1978

The only Armenian composer in our A to Z studied in Moscow. Incredibly, he managed to win a place at the Gnesin Music Academy to study the cello, even though he had never played the instrument before. He built up his reputation with works such as his Piano Concerto and Violin Concerto, as well as the ballets *Gayaneh* and *Spartacus*, the latter being his best-known piece. Prokofiev was a fan and Khachaturian held a selection of government-sponsored posts, until he wrote some music that earned the disapproval of the state, at which point he moved to writing film scores. He is seen today as having been the foremost proponent of Armenian folk music.

† **Recommended Listening:**
  Adagio from *Spartacus*

KODÁLY, ZOLTÁN
1882-1967

The son of a music-loving employee of the state railway company, Kodály's first orchestral piece was played by his school orchestra while he was still a pupil. After studying at Budapest University, he began his lifelong love affair with the folk music of Hungary and was an avid collector of tunes that had previously only been handed down by word of mouth from generation to generation. He became a good friend of fellow Hungarian composer Béla Bartók and together they indulged their passion for folk music, as well as setting up an organisation that promoted the performance of contemporary music. Kodály became an important figure in the Hungarian music scene, occupying some of the most prestigious academic music jobs in the country. Towards the end of his life, he was still travelling extensively around Europe and the USA conducting his own works.

† **Recommended Listening:**
  Háry János Suite

KREISLER, FRITZ
1875-1962

An amazing child prodigy, Kreisler entered the Vienna Conservatoire at the age of seven. He won the first prize at the Paris Conservatoire when he was still only 12 years old and was on tour by the time he was 14. He then turned his back on a career in music, opting instead to study medicine at university and then to become an officer in the Austrian army. He took up the violin again at the age of 24 and resumed his international performing career. In 1910, he gave the first performance of *Elgar's Violin Concerto* – the work is dedicated to him. He had to lay down his violin again to fight in the Austrian army in 1914, but was discharged after being wounded at the front. He was one of the first darlings of the gramophone age and his archive recordings can still be heard today. He claimed that many of the violin pieces that he composed to show off his own virtuosic playing were written by composers from the 1700s, when in fact they were all his own work.

† **Recommended Listening:**

Schön Rosmarin

L

LEHÁR, FRANZ
1870-1948

This Hungarian composer studied at the Prague Conservatoire, but learned much about music from his father, who was a military bandmaster. Despite being told by Dvořák to spend as much time as he possibly could composing, he took up roles as an orchestral violin player and working in his father's band, as well as a variety of different conducting jobs.

Lehár got his break as an operetta composer somewhat fortuitously. When the librettists of *The Merry Widow* were casting around to find a composer to set their lyrics to music, his name was suggested, though in fact he was only their second choice. He got the job when the original composer failed to come up with the goods. Lehár auditioned for the role by playing a song over the telephone. The operetta initially received a somewhat mixed reception, nearly closing before it properly opened, but eventually Lehár found that he had a hit on his hands.

† **Recommended Listening:**
Gold and Silver Waltz

LEIPZIG GEWANDHAUS ORCHESTRA

The German city of Leipzig is one of the most influential places in classical music history. The Gewandhaus was originally a Drapers' Hall, which became a concert hall way back in 1781. A new hall was built in 1884, but it was damaged by Allied bombing in 1944 and was knocked down in 1968, finally being replaced in 1981. The Orchestra's conductors over the years included Felix Mendelssohn from 1835 to 1847, while other greats have included: Wilhelm Furtwängler from 1922 to1929, Kurt Masur from 1970 to 1996, and Riccardo Chailly since 2005 – he took over the music directorship of the Leipzig Opera at the same time.

LEITMOTIV

Literally translated as 'leading motif' this is a collection of notes, a musical theme, which signifies a particular person, place or idea in an opera. So, a certain tune might be intended to represent a particular character. The theme can sometimes be repeated exactly as it has been heard before, or on other occasions it can be altered, although it remains recognisable. It is very useful for giving the audience a clue about what exactly is going on. It is particularly associated with the operas of Wagner, although many other composers use the device and it is even present in the popular musicals that are being composed today.

LEONCAVALLO, RUGGIERO
1857-1919

Born in the same year as Edward Elgar into a well-off family (his father was a police magistrate) Leoncavallo studied at the Naples Conservatoire. There was little interest in his early output as either a composer or a librettist and he ended up working as a café pianist in places as far apart as Paris, London and Egypt. Leoncavallo was hugely influenced by the operas of Wagner and set out to try to emulate his success. In 1890, though, he heard Mascagni's *Cavalleria Rusticana*, which is as unlike Wagner as anything can be imagined. It fell into the genre of what was christened verismo (realistic) opera – that is, operas that took real life as the basis for their stories. Leoncavallo's *Pagliacci* was the result. Today, it is often performed in tandem with *Cavalleria Rusticana* as a double bill (known as '*Cav & Pag*' in the trade).

Leoncavallo, though, was not as fortunate with his version of *La Bohème*. It was first performed just over a year after Puccini's immortal opera of the same name was premiered and there was only ever likely to be one winner.

† **Recommended Listening:**
  Vesti La Giubba from *Pagliacci*

LIBRETTO

This is another Italian word, which, in English, means 'little book'. Put simply, it is the book of words which are used for the sung or spoken parts of an opera. Among the most successful librettists of operatic history was Lorenzo da Ponte, who collaborated with Mozart on *The Marriage of Figaro*, *Don Giovanni* and *Cosi fan Tutte*, while Arrigo Boito, himself also a composer, wrote the libretti for Verdi's *Otello* and *Falstaff*. It is by no means an absolute rule that a composer has to work with a librettist, though. Probably the best example of a man who did it all for himself is Wagner, although this was possibly because no librettist would ever be able to match his incredibly high opinion of his own abilities.

LIEDER

The German word for 'songs' (in the singular it is *Lied*). It is not just any song though: usually (although not always), the term refers to the songs written by the German Romantic composers around the late 18th and early 19th centuries. They often set the words of great poets, such as Goethe or Schiller to music and usually (again, not always) the musical accompaniment is provided by a solo piano. Those composers who were particularly adept at writing lieder include: Schumann, Brahms, Mahler and Richard Strauss. Probably the greatest of them all was Franz Schubert, who despite his short life, churned out more than 600 separate songs. In 1815 alone, he wrote 140 and even managed eight in just one day. Among those who have made their names as singers of Lieder: the Welsh bass-baritone Bryn Terfel, who won the Lieder prize at the Cardiff Singer of the World competition, and the English tenor Ian Bostridge, whose recordings of Schubert and Schumann lieder have been acclaimed around the world.

LISZT, FRANZ
1811-1886

Taught by the composers Salieri and Czerny, Liszt was quickly singled out for his prodigious talent. He gave his first piano recital at the age of nine and was playing for kings and queens by the time he was 12. Just two years later, his first opera was produced. As an adult, he was friends with Chopin and Berlioz. He was something of a ladies' man and was a flamboyant and highly gifted performer on stage, often playing his own piano transcriptions of other people's works. He used his position as music director in Weimar both to champion the great new composers and to perform the music of the old masters, such as J.S. Bach. Despite his colourful private life, he took holy orders when he was nearly 50, although this did not seem to curb his appetite for romance wherever he travelled. As a composer, he was a major influence on other significant Romantic musicians, such as Wagner and Richard Strauss. His larger than life antics, coupled with his supreme talent, made him a hugely attractive figure.

† **Recommended Listening:**
Hungarian Rhapsody No. 2

LITOLFF, HENRY
1818-1891

Litolff was one of those people who was always destined to have an event-filled life. His mother was Scottish and his father was a dance-master prisoner-of-war from the Alsace region of France. After studying music, Litolff eloped to Gretna Green to get married at the age of 17. He separated from his wife and ended up in prison, before escaping with the assistance of the jailer's daughter. He was finally divorced and then married again, before getting divorced for a second time and married for a third time. His third wife died and – at the age of 55 – he married once again, this time to a 17-year-old. Amazingly, he also found the time to compose music and is chiefly noted for the *Scherzo* from his *Concerto Sinfonique No. 4.*

LONDON MOZART PLAYERS

The London Mozart Players, have become famous for being very good at doing one thing and doing it very well – namely, playing the music of Haydn, Mozart, Beethoven, Schubert and their contemporaries. The orchestra was founded in 1949 by the violinist Harry Blech, who set out to take the finest conductors, soloists and players to regional concert halls and small scale venues in out-of-the-way places right around the country. The Music Directors who followed on from Blech – Jane Glover, Matthias Bamert and Andrew Parrott – have each continued with this tradition. They have also maintained the purity of the London Mozart Players' central philosophy of only performing music from the Classical period. In a crowded market of London orchestras, this has given the LMP a very clear point of difference.

LONDON PHILHARMONIC ORCHESTRA

Sir Thomas Beecham founded the LPO in 1932 and the new orchestra gave its first concert at the Queen's Hall in London that same year. Just seven years later, with the outbreak of the Second World War, it ran into financial difficulties and was saved from bankruptcy only by its players, who took over its running. It has been self-governing ever since. The LPO's notable international achievements include being the first ever British orchestra to appear in Soviet Russia (in 1956) and being the first Western orchestra to visit China (in 1973). The orchestra is resident at the Royal Festival Hall in London and also spends the summer as the resident orchestra at Glyndebourne – a role it has undertaken since 1964.

The LPO is also particularly successful in the cinema, with its soundtrack recordings including *The Lord of the Rings* trilogy, *Lawrence of Arabia* and *The Mission*. After Beecham, its Principal Conductors have included Sir Adrian Boult, Sir Bernard Haitink, Sir Georg Solti, Klaus Tennstedt, Kurt Masur and the present incumbent Vladimir Jurowski – one of a new generation of young conductors who are galvanising the British orchestral scene.

LONDON SINFONIETTA

Co-founded by impresario Nicholas Snowman and conductor David Atherton in 1968, this chamber orchestra has focused on modern classical music throughout its life, with many of its performances including world premieres of key works by living composers. The orchestra has never been afraid to push the boundaries of how a classical music concert should look and sound, on occasions blending in electronic music and working with folk and jazz musicians. Other major collaborations have included pieces involving choreographed dance and specially-shot film. In 1969, the orchestra gave the premiere performance of John Tavener's *The Whale*, recording the work for The Beatles' Apple Records label the following year. Tavener ended up on the label after his brother worked as a builder on Ringo Starr's house. Today, the London Sinfonietta is resident at London's Southbank Centre and is based at King's Place, the newly built concert hall in the King's Cross area of London. It has enjoyed a particularly close relationship with the Scottish composer and conductor, Oliver Knussen.

LONDON SYMPHONY ORCHESTRA

Widely acknowledged as being among the greatest orchestras in the world, the LSO is a self-governing orchestra, which came into being in 1904 after a group of players fell out with the conductor Sir Henry Wood and resigned en masse from his Queen's Hall Orchestra. The new orchestra was owned and governed by the players, along the lines of the Berlin Philharmonic Orchestra, which had come into existence around 20 years earlier.

The LSO's first conductor was the legendary Hans Richter. In the years since, the orchestra has been conducted by a *Who's Who* of top baton-wavers including Sir Thomas Beecham, Richard Strauss, Sir John Barbirolli, Benjamin Britten, Leonard Bernstein, André Previn, Leopold Stokowski, Claudio Abbado, Sir Colin Davis, Michael Tilson Thomas and the present incumbent, Valery Gergiev.

The orchestra has mounted extensive international tours ever since it became the first British orchestra to tour abroad, to Paris, in 1906. Six years later, the LSO was the first British orchestra to visit the USA, narrowly avoiding travelling on the *Titanic*. In 1956 it was the first British orchestra to visit South Africa and, in 1963, it was the first to visit Japan. The LSO's first world tour was in 1964, taking in Israel, Turkey, Iran, India, Hong Kong, Korea, Japan and the USA.

For many people, the LSO has become synonymous with film soundtracks – it has provided the musical accompaniment to all of the *Star Wars* movies. In the late 1970s, the orchestra gained a significant financial boost from its series of *Classic Rock* recordings, which proved to be an enormous commercial success. In the strictly classical world, the LSO's recording of *Elgar's Cello Concerto*, with Jacqueline du Pré as the soloist and Sir John Barbirolli as conductor, is regarded by many as being the greatest version of the work ever committed to disc.

Today, the LSO is resident at the Barbican Centre in the City of London and at LSO St Luke's, an innovative education, rehearsal, recording and small concert venue in a converted Grade 1 listed Hawksmoor church.

LULLY, JEAN-BAPTISTE
1632-1687

Although he was Italian by birth, Lully is thought of as being a great French composer. A self-taught violinist, he worked as a servant from the age of 14, before progressing to become a dancer. In 1653 he began working for Louis XIV as a composer of ballet music. He was quickly promoted, each job slightly more important than the last, and each with a slightly grander title: Leader of the King's Violins; Instrumental Composer to the King; Superintendent of Music; Music Master to the Royal Family. The king even granted him the exclusive rights to present all opera in Paris. This gave him an enormous amount of power over all music in France; he took advantage of his grip on the country's music-making to insist on the staging of his own operas and ballets. He was also able to hire and fire musicians at will. His death is among the more bizarre in classical music: he hit his foot with the long wooden rod he used to beat time on the floor. The resulting wound became infected and he never recovered.

† **Recommended Listening:**

Alceste

M

MacCunn, Hamish
1868-1916

Something of a 'one hit wonder', Hamish MacCunn was born in Greenock and studied at the Royal College of Music, where he went on to take a teaching post when he was barely out of his teens. He tasted success early with his concert overture *The Land of the Mountain and the Flood* when he was just 21 years old. From then on, he never quite composed anything to rival it in the public's affections, but that did not stop him from working and he was much in demand as an opera conductor. He conducted the Carl Rosa Opera Company and later frequently stood in for Sir Thomas Beecham. He was a particularly ardent advocate of Scottish music. In his forties, he was appointed Head of Composition at the Guildhall School of Music. Gradually, his health deteriorated, not helped by his heavy workload of conducting, composing and teaching and he died when he was just 48 years old.

† **Recommended Listening:**
   The Land of the Mountain and the Flood

MacDowell, Edward
1860-1908

New York born, MacDowell spent 12 years living in France and Germany from the age of 16. He studied first at the Paris Conservatoire and then with the Swiss composer, Joachim Raff. His composing career really began to take off once his music was championed by Liszt. He returned to his homeland and was hailed as the new hero of American classical music. His *Piano Concerto* went down particularly well and he was appointed the first-ever Professor of Music at Columbia University in New York. He struggled to balance the demands of university life with those of being a composer and eventually gave up the job. Not long afterwards, he suffered a mental breakdown from which he never recovered. One little known fact about MacDowell: he wrote his first few pieces under the pseudonym 'Edgar Thorn'.

† **Recommended Listening:**
  To a Wild Rose

MAHLER, GUSTAV
1860-1911

The second of 14 children, Mahler's father owned a distillery in Bohemia. He owed his early success to a farm manager who heard him playing the piano and recommended him to the Vienna Conservatoire, where he studied from the age of 15. Although he studied composition and continued to play the piano, it was for his conducting that Mahler became best known during his lifetime. He achieved superstardom as a composer only long after his death.

During his early thirties, Mahler conducted concerts in all the major European centres of classical music, including Prague, Leipzig and Budapest. After converting from Judaism to Catholicism, he was appointed Conductor of the Vienna Court Opera and of the Vienna Philharmonic Orchestra. He was a massive public success, but his dedication to the task in hand made him powerful enemies. He resigned in 1907, the catalyst being the offer of the Chief Conductorship of the New York Metropolitan Opera. Though he lasted only a season there, he returned to the USA to become Music Director of the New York Philharmonic Orchestra. His workload in America was immense and, in late 1910, he was taken seriously ill. He returned to Vienna, where he died of pneumonia at the age of just 50.

At this stage, he was still best known as a conductor, and it was not until after the Second World War that his music – and particularly his nine finished symphonies – really took off. His unfinished *10th Symphony* was eventually completed from the sketches he left by musicologist Deryck Cooke.

Bruno Walter and Leonard Bernstein were two notable conductors who made it their business to introduce Mahler's music to a wider audience. Mahler himself was fascinated by the symphony, once saying to his fellow composer Sibelius: 'the symphony is a world'.

† **Recommended Listening:**

Symphony No. 8 – the Symphony of a Thousand

Mascagni, Pietro
1863-1945

Mascagni's father, an Italian baker, had his heart set on his son becoming a lawyer, but after an uncle fixed up some music lessons for the youngster he proved to be so good that he ended up at the Milan Conservatoire. His first big job was as a conductor with a touring opera company. Next, he turned his hand to composition, concentrating on complicated, innovative modern music. He changed tack for his one act opera *Cavalleria Rusticana*, which his wife entered into a competition. It won, beating 72 other composers. At this stage, Mascagni was still only 25 years old. It was produced in Rome in 1890, before being performed around the globe – at one point, *Cavalleria Rusticana* was being staged in 96 different opera houses around the world simultaneously. It made him a fortune and, although he never wrote anything else to match it, he was still reasonably successful as a composer and as a conductor.

† **Recommended Listening:**

Intermezzo from *Cavalleria Rusticana*

MASSENET, JULES
1842-1912

Among the leading opera composers in France in the latter part of the 19th century, Massenet was a child prodigy taught first by his mother and then at the Paris Conservatoire. He made his recital debut at the age of 16 and from then on paid his way by giving music lessons and by performing in cafés, bars and orchestras. When he was 21, he won the Prix de Rome, the major French composition prize. He served alongside Georges Bizet in the army during the Franco-Prussian War, before going on to make a name for himself with his operas. His major successes came in the 1880s, first with *Manon* and later with *Le Cid*. There followed a relatively unsuccessful period, even though it saw the premiere of *Werther*, now considered to be one of Massenet's greatest successes. Everything changed with *Thaïs*, which proved to be an enduring hit.

† **Recommended Listening:**
  Meditation from *Thaïs*

MASTER OF THE QUEEN'S (KING'S) MUSICK

The role dates back to the reign of Charles I, when Nicholas Lanier, a composer and lute player, became the first to hold the job from 1626 until the post was abolished by Oliver Cromwell. He returned to it in 1660 when Charles II regained the throne. The position involved accompanying the monarch on his travels, as well as leading his private band of musicians, which, during Charles II's reign, numbered 24 string players. Other holders of the title have included William Boyce (from 1775), John Stanley (from 1779), Edward Elgar (from 1924), Arnold Bax (from 1942) and Arthur Bliss (from 1953). The present incumbent is the Salford-born composer, Sir Peter Maxwell Davies, who has been a popular and well respected holder of the post.

McCartney, Paul
1942-

Having been at the very top of the pop music tree since the 1960s, Paul McCartney successfully made the move into classical music in the 1990s. His first major classical work was Paul McCartney's *Liverpool Oratorio*, a collaboration with Carl Davis, to celebrate the Royal Liverpool Philharmonic Society's 150th anniversary. It received its premiere at Liverpool Cathedral in 1991 and the subsequent album recording features the sopranos Kiri Te Kanawa and Sally Burgess, the tenor Jerry Hadley and the bass-baritone Willard White, performing alongside the Royal Liverpool Philharmonic Orchestra and the choir of Liverpool Cathedral. McCartney's other classical works include: *Standing Stone* (1997), featuring the London Symphony Orchestra conducted by Lawrence Foster; *Working Classical* (1999), a collection of short classical pieces, some of which are based on his earlier pop compositions; and *Ecce Cor Meum* (2006), an oratorio in four movements that won the Best Album category at the 2007 Classical Brit Awards. The title is Latin for 'Behold My Heart'.

† **Recommended Listening:**
  A Leaf from *Working Classical*

Mendelssohn, Felix
1809-1847

Mendelssohn was born into a wealthy Hamburg family and showed plenty of early musical talent. In 1825, the composer Cherubini spotted his true potential, but said 'he puts too much material into his coat' – a warning to be careful about not cramming too many musical ideas into each piece.

At the age of 16, Mendelssohn wrote his *Octet*, which is still considered to be one of the greatest classical music works ever composed by a teenager. He followed the success of the *Octet* with his *Overture to*

A Midsummer Night's Dream, although it took him a further 17 years to complete the rest of the incidental music.

Mendelssohn was a big fan of Bach and when he was 20, he organised performances of Bach's *St. Matthew Passion* to mark its centenary. This was unusual because Bach was highly unfashionable at the time; it was the first time the *St. Matthew Passion* had been performed since Bach's death in 1750. He also revived the music of Franz Schubert, giving the premiere of his last symphony when it was rediscovered more than a decade after the older composer's death.

He then got the travelling bug, journeying around Europe and spending a lot of time in Britain, with Scotland being a particular favourite destination. While he was there, he developed the ideas behind his *Hebrides Overture* and *Scottish Symphony*.

He became a favourite of the Royal family, regularly meeting Queen Victoria and Prince Albert. He was also lionised by music societies and festivals across the country – his oratorio *Elijah* received its premiere during the Birmingham Festival.

As well as composing, Mendelssohn was a respected conductor. He became music director of the Leipzig Gewandhaus Orchestra at the age of only 26. He also founded a major music school in the city, persuading his fellow composers Ignaz Moscheles and Robert Schumann to join him on the staff.

† **Recommended Listening:**
Violin Concerto

MENUHIN, YEHUDI
1916-1999

Born in New York, Menuhin was a classic child prodigy: music lessons from the age of five; a professional violin recital at seven; concerto performances by the time he was nine. Menuhin was not only technically highly proficient as a child, his interpretations were seen as being very special in themselves – his performance of *Beethoven's Violin Concerto* when he was 11 years old is still regarded as one of the great renditions of the work.

Menuhin's family moved to Paris in the 1930s, with the teenager performing in a duo with his sister Hephzibah, who played piano. At the age of 18 he undertook a world tour, before allowing himself a two year sabbatical in California at the house he had purchased in Los Gatos, high on a hill overlooking the Santa Clara Valley. Even though he had homes in Gstaad and London, throughout his life Menuhin preferred to call himself a citizen of the world, always going back to Los Gatos at least once a year. So the story goes, he would drive around in a V12 Cadillac, with white-walled tyres – a time he always referred to as his 'carefree days'.

During the Second World War, Menuhin gave around 500 performances for Allied troops and in 1944 he was the first artist to perform at the Paris Opera after the city's liberation from the Nazis. With the coming of peace, his fame continued to grow. He became interested in yoga and was influential in raising its profile in the UK. He also started his own school in Stoke D'Abernon in Surrey in 1963. It quickly became one of the pre-eminent music schools in the world, with alumni including Tasmin Little, Nicola Benedetti and Nigel Kennedy.

Aside from his classical violin playing, Menuhin loved Indian music and jazz. He had a long professional partnership with the jazz fiddler, Stephane Grapelli. He was also an accomplished conductor, enjoying long associations with the Bath Festival.

MODERN PERIOD

With the dawn of the 20th century, the Romantic period was drawing to a close. Many composers now seemed to be at a loss as to what to do next with music. There was almost a feeling that everything had been done in terms of musical development, and that, with the death of Wagner, an era had come to an end.

Many composers decided that a young Austrian, called Arnold Schoenberg, was right to start everything all over again. He developed entirely new rules for how you might use harmony, melody and rhythm: a system he called '12 tone music' or 'serialism.' (Its principle feature is to make each of the 12 tones of a chromatic scale equal.) Serialism won an immediate following at the time, starting with Schoenberg's pupils. They became known as the Second Viennese School, its main proponents being Anton Webern and Alban Berg. The style gained momentum as the century progressed, not least due to Schoenberg's teaching when he took up residence in the USA.

Schoenberg's methods were by no means universally accepted, though. Stravinsky, for one, adopted as much or as little of them as he needed, sometimes incorporating 12 tone, sometimes not. Richard Strauss, while also being starkly modernist, was not interested in serialism at all, preferring instead to push his own brand of tonality to its limits. Many other composers, who had been around from the middle half of the 19th century, preferred to continue in the traditional manner, seeing nothing wrong with keys and tonality. Puccini, Elgar and Rachmaninov were just a few of the composers who continued to plough the Romantic furrow in a modernist field.

Of course, good old fashioned tunes and harmonies have survived intact throughout the 20th century, thanks to composers such as Vaughan Williams, Holst and Britten in Britain, Rodrigo in Spain, the composers who called themselves '*Les Six*' in France and, to some extent, the likes of Copland in the USA.

Come the 21st century and tonality is still alive and well. Minimalism is still thriving, as is a rediscovered neo-classicism, a whole raft of composers working alongside contemporary film composers using an audience-friendly musical language. Many of these composers, such as Karl Jenkins, Howard Goodall and John Rutter, have their own entries in our A to Z. Other well-respected contemporary composers include:

James MacMillan (born 1959): possibly the best-known Scottish composer of his generation. His *Veni, Veni, Emmanuel*, a concerto for percussion first performed in 1992 by Evelyn Glennie, is considered a modern classic.

Judith Weir (born 1954): a former pupil of John Tavener, the opera house and theatre are ideal places to experience her fresh, modern sounds.

George Benjamin (born 1960): studied with Messiaen before having an early 'modern' hit with *Ringed by the Flat Horizon*.

Gavin Bryars (born 1943): the most famous (and quite possibly the only famous) composer from Goole in East Yorkshire. His *Jesus Blood Never Failed Me Yet* was a big hit in the mid-1990s.

Mark-Anthony Turnage (born 1960): another man at home with theatre music. His music to Steven Berkoff's *Greek* is breathtaking.

MONTEVERDI, CLAUDIO
1567-1643

He may have been born well over 400 years ago, but Monteverdi was one of a group of composers who were quietly revolutionary in the way that they wrote their music. They broke many of the accepted rules of the time and did much to develop the way in which music was composed. History has judged Monteverdi to have been particularly influential in the development of opera, although he began by composing madrigals. He was a master at bringing emotion into his music and also at creating a sense of drama around what he wrote. Arguably, he was among the first composers to ensure that the music he wrote matched the words being sung, making his songs more natural in their style than many of those that had been written before. His first opera was *La favola d'Orfeo*, which featured a score written for a full-size orchestra, which was unusual at the time.

† **Recommended Listening:**
   Vespers

MOZART, LEOPOLD
1719-1787

He may come first in our A to Z, but Leopold's greatest musical creation was undoubtedly his son, who follows in the next entry. A composer and violinist, Leopold was a member of the orchestra belonging to the Prince-Archbishop of Salzburg. In 1762, he was promoted to court composer. As a child, his daughter Anna (known to the family as Nannerl) often performed alongside her brother Wolfgang. They were quite an act and Leopold spent a good deal of time and effort promoting the young duo both as a money-making enterprise and also as a means of gaining access to the palaces of the nobility right across Europe.

† **Recommended Listening:**
  Toy Symphony

MOZART, WOLFGANG AMADEUS
1756-1791

Mozart is the composer for all seasons, with his music often hailed as being the greatest in each of the areas of classical music in which he wrote. Operas, symphonies, concertos, choral works, chamber music, solo piano – the list goes on. His success is largely due to his genius, his amazing volume of output, and his ability to write the most perfect form of classical music in all genres. It is also, partly at least, down to his having been writing at the right time – smack bang in the middle of the era of eras: the Classical period. At this time, classical music was still free from the storms of the Romantics. He also died young and, as with many other musical greats who have met the same fate, his early passing seemed to allow an air of mystery and intrigue to develop around him in the years after his death.

Mozart was born in 1756 and lived for just 35 years. He was a native of Salzburg and spent a good deal of his early life travelling. As soon as his ambitious father, Leopold, realised just how phenomenal and prodigious Mozart's musical talent actually was, the young boy was propelled around Europe for years at a time. In today's musical world, he would have been seen to have delivered a highly successful European promotional tour.

Despite being awash with child prodigies around this time, Europe – particularly its nobility – was quick to marvel at the Mozart phenomenon. The impact was such that, when he was an adult, Mozart was not always taken seriously because the memory of a child doing musical tricks was hard to shake off.

After the age of 19, Mozart toured in his own right, with just his mother for company. He was growing too big for Salzburg; he needed a bigger musical canvas upon which to work. So, he moved to Vienna, effectively as a freelance composer, taking work where he could find it. Here he married Constanze Weber. It was a very happy marriage, despite

MOZART'S LETTERS

One of the most amazing non-musical legacies of any composer, Mozart's surviving letters span a 22-year period from his teens to just before his death. What they reveal very much counterbalances the traditional portrait of an angelic genius. The Mozart of the letters is coarse, rude, childish and apparently badly schooled in grammar (no doubt partly to do with his touring childhood). His obsession with his, and others', nether regions is undeniable and, while their reading might make some uncomfortable, they show a very 'humanising' side to a great mind. Comments such as the one written while he was composing *The Magic Flute* 'Today, out of absolute tedium, I wrote an aria for the opera', serve to shed light on Mozart the man, possibly helping us to appreciate him all the more.

the fact that Mozart had pursued Constanze's sister for some years. In Vienna, he continued to compose a huge amount of music, including symphonies, piano concertos and operas, possibly the purest yet riskiest musical currency of all at the time.

The *Marriage of Figaro* and *Così fan tutte* were both premiered in Vienna to great popular acclaim. Mozart was also popular in Prague, where he premiered his opera *Don Giovanni* as well as masterpieces such as the *Jupiter Symphony (No.41)* and *Eine Kleine Nachtmusik*.

In the final year of his life, Mozart wrote *The Magic Flute*, the *Ave Verum Corpus*, the *Clarinet Concerto* and part of a *Requiem*. He died not quite penniless but, certainly, with cash problems and was buried in an unmarked pauper's grave.

† **Recommended Listening:**

Piano Concerto No. 20 in D Minor
Voi Che Sapete from The Marriage of Figaro
Symphony No. 41 'Jupiter'

MOZART'S ENGLAND

While Vienna was definitely the city of Mozart's dreams, it is possible to find traces of the genius on these shores:

180 EBURY STREET, LONDON: A plaque denotes Mozart 'composed his first symphony here in 1764'. He would have been eight.

19 CECIL COURT, LONDON: Mozart lodged here with a barber.

21 FRITH STREET (THEN THRIFT ST.), LONDON: There is still a plaque opposite Ronnie Scott's Famous Jazz Club, marking the place where he also lodged.

BOURNE PARK, NEAR CANTERBURY, KENT: Mozart stayed in this wonderful Queen Anne House to attend the races at nearby Barham Downs.

🎼 MOZART, WOLFGANG AMADEUS

1756	Born Salzburg, Austria
1761	Appears as a keyboard performer for the first time
1762	Travels to Munich and Vienna, where he and his sister appear at the Bavarian and Austrian courts
1763-66	First European tour, including visits to Paris, London and Italy
1772	Becomes Kapellmeister to the Cardinal-Archbishop of Salzburg
1777-79	Dismissed by the archbishop, Mozart visits Mannheim and Paris before returning to Salzburg to patch things up with his patron
1781	Visiting Vienna with the archbishop, Mozart quarrels with him again and is dismissed for the second time. He becomes a freelance musician
1782	Marries Constanze Weber. He writes his opera *Die Entfuhrung aus dem Serail* (*The Abduction from the Harem*) and begins composing his mature piano concertos, quartets and symphonies
1786-87	Premieres of *Le Nozze di Figaro* and *Don Giovanni* in Vienna and Prague respectively
1788-89	Composes his last three symphonies
1791	Mozart premieres his last piano concerto and his final two operas, *La Clemenza di Tito* (*The Mercy of Titus*) and *Die Zauberflote* (*The Magic Flute*). He starts work on his *Requiem* but dies before finishing it

MUSSORGSKY, MODEST
1839-1881

One of the group of five Russian nationalist composers known as the 'Mighty Handful', Mussorgsky started out his adult life as an army officer, but eventually he turned to a musical career, combining composing with working as a low-grade civil servant. A lifelong drinker, he eventually became an alcoholic and, probably for this reason, seemed to lack the ability to actually finish many of his compositions. He started and stopped work on two earlier operas, for instance, before eventually composing *Boris Godunov*, now hailed as his operatic masterpiece.

Mussorgsky is also famous for his orchestral study *A Night on a Bare Mountain* and also for his piano work *Pictures at an Exhibition*. However, neither of the versions of this that we know today are all his own work – indeed *A Night on a Bare Mountain* was not premiered until after the composer's death. His great friend Rimsky-Korsakov re-orchestrated it (as he did much of *Boris Godunov*), while it was the French composer Maurice Ravel who later turned *Pictures at an Exhibition* into the orchestral showpiece that tends to be played today.

† **Recommended Listening:**

The Hut on a Hen's Legs and *The Great Gate of Kiev*
from *Pictures at an Exhibition*

N

NATIONALISM

While it is true to say that nationalism has been around for as long as there have been nations, the main period during which it flourished was the 19th century, often alongside, and as a bi-product of, political movements for change. In the musical world, it is often pithily labelled 'patriotism in music'. It is the desire by composers to reflect audibly, to varying extents, the nations in which they were born. The idea is that the listener will be able to hear the nationality in the music. Sometimes this is achieved by the use of traditional folk songs, tunes and rhythms, which are incorporated into the music. On other occasions, composers simply write their own material in the style of their country's traditional music.

RUSSIAN NATIONALISM

In Russia, musical nationalism was fathered by Glinka, one of the first Russian composers to achieve any sort of fame outside his own country. He was born into a wealthy, land-owning family and he first discovered his latent nationalism when he was abroad, homesick in Italy. When he returned, he wrote *A Life for the Tsar*, the first major Russian opera, which, according to one commentator, 'marked the boundary between the past and the future of Russian music'.

A group of younger composers, based in St. Petersburg, continued where Glinka left off. Dubbed 'The Five' or the 'Mighty Handful', they were led by Balakirev (the group's other members were Cui, Mussorgsky, Rimsky-Korsakov and Borodin). Largely self-taught, their works, often infused with folk music, served to make Russia a thriving centre of the

19th-century musical universe. Borodin's *Prince Igor*, Mussorgsky's *A Night on a Bare Mountain* and Rimsky-Korsakov's *Scheherazade* are all great examples of their work.

Interestingly, though, Tchaikovsky, the other great Russian composer of the time, preferred to stand apart. Indeed, 'The Five' did not consider him to be a nationalist. Despite this, many of his compositions – the opera *Eugene Onegin*, the orchestral *Marche Slave* and the *1812 Overture*, for instance – sound hugely nationalistic to our ears today.

SCANDINAVIAN NATIONALISM

In Norway and Finland, Grieg and Sibelius were both musical firebrands in their countries' respective nationalist movements. Under the influence of the Norwegian violinist and folk historian Ole Bull, Grieg composed a huge body of music, particularly for the piano, in the national style. He is best remembered for works such as *Peer Gynt*, written as incidental music for Henrik Ibsen's fairy-tale play. Sibelius's music is all totally original, but yet Finnish-sounding. He became a hero of Finland's struggle for full independence from Tsarist Russia with tone poems like *Finlandia*, which occupies the same place in Finnish hearts as *Land of Hope and Glory* does in England or *Men of Harlech* does in Wales.

CZECH NATIONALISM

Czech, Bohemian, Moravian and Slovakian nationalism all tends to be clubbed together in a group. At the head of the movement was Smetana, from Bohemia, who scored an early success with his second Czech opera *The Bartered Bride*, into which he incorporated genuine folk melodies and dances. His later work *Má Vlast* ('*My Fatherland*') is a set of six, separate symphonic poems each depicting some aspect of his homeland, the most famous being *Vltava*, a musical portrait of the Moldau river. Dvořák championed the cause with his *Slavonic Dances* and *Slavonic Rhapsodies*, whilst Janáček, a fervent advocate of his native Moravian music, contributed to the cause in the 20th century with works like his opera, *Jenufa*.

NEW YORK PHILHARMONIC ORCHESTRA

The USA's oldest symphony orchestra was founded in 1842 – almost 40 years before the next oldest American ensemble. For a period from 1928, it was known as the Philharmonic-Symphony Orchestra of New York, following a merger with the New York Symphony Orchestra. The role of the New York Philharmonic's Music Director is among the most coveted in classical music, with previous holders of the post including Gustav Mahler, Arturo Toscanini, Sir John Barbirolli, Leopold Stokowski, Leonard Bernstein, Pierre Boulez, Zubin Mehta, Kurt Masur and Lorin Maazel. The current Music Director is Alan Gilbert.

NOCTURNE

Taken from the French word meaning 'of the night', the first composer to use the term was in fact an Irishman, John Field. He wrote a series of 20 short studies for solo piano, which had a gently romantic late night feeling about them. They are rather dreamy pieces, with floating chords being played by the pianist's left hand, while the right plays an expressive, sometimes melancholy melody. The idea was quickly taken up by Chopin who wrote a total of 21 nocturnes.

NORTHERN SINFONIA

Founded by Michael Hall in 1958, this chamber orchestra was originally known as the 'Sinfonia Orchestra'. A year later, 'Northern' was added to the front of the name. Later still, 'Orchestra' was dropped from the band's title.

The orchestra was resident at Newcastle City Hall until 2004, when it moved to its stunning new home, The Sage Gateshead, on the other side of the River Tyne. Designed by Lord Foster, this futuristic building contains two acoustically excellent concert halls, another hall which is used for rehearsals and a 25-room music education centre. It has enjoyed artistically strong relationships with a series of impressive conducting talents, including Tamas Vasary, Iván Fischer, and the current Music Director Thomas Zehetmair.

NYMAN, MICHAEL
1944-

A prolific and commercially successful British composer, Michael Nyman studied at the Royal Academy of Music in the 1960s, where his compositions at the time were at the cutting edge of new music. He went on to study at King's College in London, where he turned back the clock, specialising in 17th century musicology. He put composing on the back-burner for a while, concentrating on musicology and also on music criticism. While he was writing for The Spectator, he became the first critic to use the term 'Minimalism' when writing about the music of Steve Reich and Philip Glass. Gradually, he spent more time writing music than writing words, forming a highly successful professional partnership with the film director Peter Greenaway, which saw him composing soundtracks for movies such as *The Draughtsman's Contract* and *The Cook, The Thief, His Wife and Her Lover*.

† **Recommended Listening:**

The Piano

O

OBOE

A member of the woodwind family, the oboe is the instrument to which all others in the orchestra tune. This is because it can easily be heard above the rest and also because it holds its note well. It gets its name from the French words *haut* (high) and *bois* (wood). To play, the oboist blows through a double reed, uncovering or covering the six holes on the instrument's body. The metal attachments (which look a little like jewellery) allow the player to open and close the holes with ease. The oboe's interior chamber is conical, rather than cylindrical like flutes and clarinets, and this gives it its unique sound.

The instrument has been a popular choice for concerto composers; Vivaldi, Albinoni and Mozart wrote particularly fine examples. In more modern times, Ravel wrote a starring role for the oboe in his celebrated *Boléro*, while Richard Strauss's *Oboe Concerto* was one of his last masterpieces.

† **Recommended Listening:**
   Malabar Jasmine from *The Flower Clock* by Jean Françaix

OFFENBACH, JACQUES
1819-1880

Offenbach's musical career started in 1833 at the age of 14 when his father took him to Paris and got him admitted as a cello student at the Conservatoire. It was at this time that the teenage Offenbach changed his first name from Jacob to Jacques. His surname was not his original one either. Offenbach's father, a cantor at a Cologne synagogue, altered it when he renamed himself after the town of his birth.

After completing his studies, Offenbach junior became a cello virtuoso, before turning to conducting and becoming a prime mover in the development of operetta (he wrote more than 100 of them). In the process, he cemented his position as one of the most popular composers of the 19th century, churning out crowd-pleasing music with memorable tunes.

† **Recommended Listening:**

Barcarolle from *The Tales of Hoffmann*

OPERA

The word opera is the plural of the Latin word *opus* (work). It originates from the phrase *opera in musica*, which means 'musical works', but over the years it has been shortened.

Put at its simplest, opera is the combination of singing, drama and musical accompaniment, a genre whereby the music and the plot are as one. This is what differentiates them from musicals, which generally speaking are dramas with breaks for musical numbers. In an opera, the drama and the music are not separated in the same way.

Opera in the form that we know it began to take shape in the dying years of the 16th century. It was the idea of a group of arts-loving intellectuals known as the Florentine Camerata. They wanted to resurrect Greek drama, with music, and the first offering came from a composer and singer called Jacopo Peri. Most musical historians consider his work *Dafne*, written around 1597 and now lost, to be the first real opera. Peri went on to write the second ever opera, *Euridice*, which is not lost, but simply no longer performed.

It is an opera by Monteverdi that is the oldest still to hold the stage. By coincidence, it is on the same subject as Peri's second opera: the story of Orpheus and Eurydice. Monteverdi simply called it *La favola d'Orfeo*. It was the real starting point for a brand new genre of music which continues to thrive to this day.

Baroque Opera

The elder Scarlatti, Lully and Rameau all quickly got to grips with the new format. Scarlatti alone wrote well over 100 different operas. He is considered the father of the Neapolitan opera school. Purcell's *Dido and Aeneas*, from 1689, is a landmark in English opera. For some people, no composer has ever bettered the hauntingly beautiful aria *When I am Laid in Earth*. Handel, having learnt the operatic trade in Italy, wrote 40 or so operas for Britain in his 30s. Many of them were premiered at London's Covent Garden.

Mozart Operas

To Mozart, opera was the finest medium in which a composer could operate. It is not surprising, then, that he contributed works which are still thought of as being the creation of a genius. He wrote three works with the librettist Lorenzo da Ponte (*The Marriage of Figaro*, *Don Giovanni* and *Così fan tutte*). Many musical historians believe that these operas have never been bettered for the synthesis of singers and orchestra, not to mention melodic beauty and level of invention.

Bel Canto

Bel Canto opera is generally considered to be opera in the Italian style, written in the early 19th century, a time when singers became superstars. It seems as if audiences of the time could not get enough of these showy, coloratura classics, where sopranos were given the chance to impress with their fast, agile singing. Donizetti's *Lucia di Lammermoor* and Bellini's *Norma* are both masterpieces of this type of opera.

Verdi, Puccini and Wagner

The three towering figures in late Romantic opera all specialised in their chosen discipline and rarely wrote anything else. Verdi's work is in a direct line from that of Donizetti, with an emphasis on increased drama and a huge wealth of tunes. Puccini's brand of *verismo* opera (telling real life stories) was often considered near scandalous; as late as the 1950s, his Tosca was described by one critic as 'a shabby little shocker'. Wagner is a standalone giant in the opera world, taking the form to its absolute limit. He did away with the idea of having a recitative (a form of speech-like singing) and then an aria, instead blending the whole opera into one continuous, overflowing bath of musical delight.

ORATORIO

The word comes from the Latin word *oratio* (prayer). Today, oratorio means a work for chorus, soloists and orchestra, usually, though not always, with a religious text and intended to be performed in church or in a concert hall.

What is generally reckoned to be the first true oratorio, Emilio De'Cavalieri's 'sacred opera' *Rappresentatione di Anima et Di Corpo*, dates from 1600, though the story is 50 years or so older. St. Filippo Neri, an Italian priest, had the idea of what can best be described as moral musical entertainments. He won the backing of the Jesuits for his notion. After De'Cavalieri, Giacomo Carissimi, another Italian, developed the form; one of his pupils, Marc-Antoine Charpentier, took it to France. In Germany, Heinrich Schutz was oratorio's foremost pioneer.

Some great oratorio composers include:

Handel: He was chiefly known as a composer of Italian-style operas when he wrote his first oratorio in 1707. From that point on, he became a master of the genre. His most famous work, *Messiah* – written for a 1742 Dublin premiere – is just the tip of the iceberg. Handel wrote 29 oratorios on religious and secular subjects, ranging from *Saul and Solomon* to *Susanna and Samson*.

Mendelssohn: Although he only completed two oratorios, Mendelssohn was at the forefront of an oratorio revival in the 19th century. His oratorios *St. Paul* and *Elijah* are still in the repertoire today.

Elgar: Oratorios flourished in late Victorian Britain, with Elgar's *The Dream of Gerontius* quite possibly the jewel in the imperial crown. He also wrote *The Apostles*, *The Kingdom* and *The Light of Life*.

ORCHESTRA

The word 'orchestra' did not originally mean a group of people playing music at all. Instead, it was the place where the group stood or sat. In a Greek amphitheatre, the natural slope of the seats was called the 'Koilon', the backdrop to the stage was known as the 'Scena', and the semi-circular piece of flat ground between the two was the 'Orchestra'. Eventually, it came to mean the people who played there, too.

The modern orchestra, like the ancient one before it, was also born in the theatre, originally to accompany plays and operas. The Dresden Staatskapelle is the world's oldest, tracing its origins back as far as 1548. It was soon joined by others, as churches, courts, cities and towns across Europe founded their own orchestras over the next couple of centuries. The virtuoso Mannheim orchestra (run by the local Elector) was particularly important in advancing the cause. The UK's oldest surviving symphony orchestra is the Royal Liverpool Philharmonic Orchestra, which was founded in 1840 and became a fully-professional band in 1853.

ORCHESTRATION

Orchestration is the part of a composer's job that comes after the initial composing itself. Once the central ideas have been created, the art of sorting out who plays what is called 'orchestration'. Many composers consider it a completely separate procedure, and some are thought of as being greater masters of the process than others. Ravel, Berlioz and Dukas, for example, are all considered experts in the field.

Rimsky-Korsakov was another such expert, making a habit of superbly orchestrating virtually everything that he laid his hands on. He was already strong in the area of orchestration while he was still at college, writing musical arrangements for the student band. He perfected his craft while he was in the navy, when he made a point of learning how to play just about every instrument of the orchestra.

Wagner is worthy of a mention in this section, too. When he could not get quite the right combination of orchestral colours to do justice to the sound that was in his head, he simply invented his own instrument to create it. The 'Wagner Tuba' was the result. It is, in fact, more of a big horn than a tuba. Wagner employed it to great musical effect in his mammoth four-opera cycle, The Ring.

THE MAKE-UP OF THE ORCHESTRA

The biggest section of an orchestra is made up of string instruments. In a standard-sized symphony orchestra, you might find around 30 violinists, a dozen or so violas, maybe ten cellos and around eight double basses. That is a total of around sixty or so players in all – roughly two thirds of the band. The reason that these numbers are not exact is that different composers call for slightly different musical configurations for each of their works.

The brass section typically comprises three trumpets, three trombones, four French horns and a tuba – allowing the composer to paint musical pictures in with three high, four middle, three low and one very low brush. The brass section is undoubtedly loud: these 11 players alone can often drown out the entire string section because of the sheer volume of sound that their instruments produce.

Next up are the woodwind instruments, which are not necessarily made of wood these days. This section is made up of two or three flutes, a piccolo, a couple of oboes, four clarinets and perhaps a bass clarinet, two bassoons and possibly a contra-bassoon. The final part of the orchestra is a percussion section of three or four players, playing various instruments such as timpani, cymbals, side drums, bass drums, xylophones and triangles. One or sometimes two harpists and a pianist, who might play the celesta when required, more or less completes the complement of a full standard symphony orchestra.

ORFF, CARL

A Munich-born composer and academic, Orff's popularity today rests almost solely on his 'scenic cantata', *Carmina Burana*. It was written when he was 42 and is a setting of the often licentious poems of some medieval monks. After its success, Orff disowned his earlier music. He continued to write more in the same style, often using speech-like rhythms with an almost minimalist approach to melody and harmony. Simultaneously, he continued his pioneering work in musical education.

Orff was criticised during and after the Second World War for his ambivalent relationship with the Nazis, who had hailed *Carmina Burana* as 'the kind of clear, stormy and yet always disciplined music that our time requires'. In 1939, he agreed to write new incidental music for Shakespeare's *A Midsummer Night's Dream* to replace Mendelssohn's, which the Nazis had banned.

ORGAN

The organ is a monster of an instrument, often employing up to five keyboards (known as manuals), a pedal board and sometimes more than a hundred stops. Although born in ancient Greece (where water was often used to create the necessary pressure), it was in the sixth and seventh centuries that an air-bellowed version of the organ began to come into its own. By Bach's time, a golden age of organ building had led to a mass of complex music being written for what was then regarded as a high-tech instrument.

Royal Albert Hall organ: the organ was overhauled and rebuilt in 2002. It has 147 stops and an amazing 9,997 pipes.

Westminster Abbey organ: the current Westminster Abbey organ has 5 manuals and 109 stops, and was first used at the coronation of George VI.

OVERTURE

Overtures started off life as short pieces played before the opera house curtain rose on the main business of the evening. In many cases, they were little more than a medley of the tunes that were to appear later in the opera proper.

In the Romantic era, the overture developed an existence of its own as a stand-alone piece of orchestral music. Such overtures are occasionally called 'concert overtures' to differentiate them from their pre-dramatic counterparts and are often similar in style to the later 'symphonic poem' or 'tone poem'. From Mozart's opera overtures, through Rossini's and Verdi's and on to the concert overtures by Beethoven, Berlioz, Mendelssohn and Brahms, the overture remains one of the most approachable forms of orchestral music around.

P

PACHELBEL, JOHANN
1653-1706
As well as being a significant composer, Nuremburg-born Pachelbel was a virtuoso organist, his talents winning him the top job at St. Stephen's, Vienna's great cathedral, as well as in Eisenach and Stuttgart. In Eisenach, he grew close to the Bach family and was eventually godfather to one of Johann Sebastian's children. The composer of countless pieces of music in varied forms, his life was scarred by tragedy: his wife and child both died of the plague. He is remembered now only for one work, albeit a beautiful one: his *Canon in D*.

† **Recommended Listening:**
Canon in D

PAGANINI, NICCOLÒ
1782-1840
Even in a period stuffed with musical prodigies, Paganini appears to have been something of a wonder. The greatest violin virtuoso of the previous generation, Alessandro Rolla, said he could teach the Genoa-born youngster nothing more by the time he had reached the age of 12. Paganini's phenomenal technique had firmly established him as a great solo artist by the time he was 27. He toured first Italy then all around Europe, writing his own concertos to display his amazing skills. When rumours abounded that he must be in league with the Devil to be so accomplished, Paganini himself did little to deny the myth. He commissioned Berlioz to write the symphony *Harold in Italy*, though he

initially rejected it because he felt that the solo viola part was not showy enough. Later, he apologised and embraced it wholeheartedly. His later life was marred by bad health and ill-judged financial investments.

† **Recommended Listening:**
Violin Concerto No. 2

PALESTRINA, GIOVANNI PIERLUIGI DA
c. 1525-1594

This Italian composer took his name from Palestrina, the pleasant hillside town near Rome, where he was born. Chiefly a choral writer, Palestrina followed his employer, the Bishop of Palestrina, to Rome when the Bishop became Pope

Julius III. He initially worked at the Capella Giulia, as choirmaster. After taking on several other influential choral posts, he returned to the Capella Giulia as its overall director at the age of 46. Following the death of his wife and sons, and a brief (but rather half-hearted) flirtation with the priesthood, he married the wealthy widow of a furrier, and spent his happy later years, more than comfortably off, publishing collections of his music.

† **Recommended Listening:**
Missa Papae Marcelli

PARRY, HUBERT
1848-1918

Sir Charles Hubert Hastings Parry was very much a man of his age. After Eton and Oxford (he completed his music degree at the age of 18 while still at Eton), he became an underwriter at Lloyds of London. Following seven years in the City, studying music in his spare time, he gave up business for composition – earning extra money writing articles for the august Grove's *Dictionary of Music and Musicians*, the first volume of which was published in 1878.

Parry taught successfully for many years, his star pupils including Vaughan Williams and Holst. His own compositions rapidly put him at the head of the musical establishment and his large-scale choral works, notably *I Was Glad* and *Blest Pair of Sirens*, are still staples of the repertoire. He is probably best-known, however, for his *Jerusalem*. In 1916, he set Blake's visionary poem to music for 'Fight for the Right,' a woman's suffrage movement. Some years later, Elgar re-orchestrated the piece and it is this version that is still sung at the Last Night of the Proms every year. When he heard it, George V is said to have remarked that he wished it could take the place of the National Anthem.

† **Recommended Listening:**
 Jerusalem

Pärt, Arvo
1935-

The only Estonian composer in our A to Z, Pärt studied in the country's capital city, Talinn, doubling up as a recording engineer for Estonian Radio and writing film music in his free time. Early on, he was considered one of the firebrands of modern Estonian music, before entering two periods of self-imposed silence. The first came about as the result of the banning of his *Credo* by the Soviet regime and the second resulted from his decision to transform his musical style. As a result, his music became minimalist and ethereal, reflecting Pärt's passion for plainchant. Soon, he became well-known for what he called his 'tintinnabuli' pieces, hypnotic works in which there are very few notes and the music is saturated with bell-like motifs. Indeed, Pärt's word for them comes from the Latin for 'little bells'.

† **Recommended Listening:**
 Spiegel im Spiegel

PERCUSSION

Percussion instruments are struck by a stick, a hand or a pedal. They are generally thought to be the second oldest instruments on the planet, only beaten by the voice. The percussion family can be divided into two parts: those instruments with a set pitch and those without. Examples of the former include timpani, xylophones and glockenspiels, while triangles, tambourines and castanets fall into the second category. There are a whole host of other weird and wonderful objects which composers have dreamed up for the percussion section to play, including car horns and assorted pieces of metal in different shapes and sizes.

For a long time, percussion instruments tended to be used in Western classical music more for colour, rhythm and other specific musical effects than for anything else. However, over recent years, they have emerged as instruments in their own right. Artists such as Evelyn Glennie and Colin Currie have done an enormous amount to raise percussionists' standing and also to grow the repertoire through the commissioning of new, often spectacular works.

PHILHARMONIA ORCHESTRA

The Philharmonia Orchestra's fine reputation is all the more impressive given its relative youth. It was the brainchild of impresario and record company executive Walter Legge, who came up with the plan to establish a new virtuoso orchestra towards the end of the Second World War. It made its debut on 27 October, 1945, in London's Kingsway Hall, with Sir Thomas Beecham conducting.

The connection between Beecham and the orchestra did not last for long – he disagreed with Legge over how it should be run and decided to form his own Royal Philharmonic – but other leading figures flocked to conduct it. Within a few years, the orchestra, which Legge had formed primarily to record for EMI, was being conducted by no less a personage than Richard Strauss. It went on to give the world premiere of his *Four*

Last Songs for soprano and orchestra in 1950. During that decade, the orchestra blossomed further, taking part in the historic opening concert of London's Royal Festival Hall in 1951 and touring Europe and the USA with Herbert von Karajan in 1952 and 1954 respectively.

In 1964, Legge decided to disband the orchestra. It refused to die, instead re-emerging as the self-governing New Philharmonia Orchestra. The legendary conductor Otto Klemperer, whom Legge had appointed principal conductor of the Philharmonia in 1959, decided to stick by the players, as did other great conductors, notably Carlo Maria Giulini. Klemperer remained closely associated with the orchestra until his retirement in 1971. The new name stuck until 1977, when it was changed back to the Philharmonia Orchestra.

During the 1970s and 1980s, an amazing variety of conducting talents stepped onto the Philharmonia's podium: Simon Rattle, Lorin Maazel, Vladimir Ashkenazy, Ricardo Muti and Bernard Haitink were among the number. Plácido Domingo even chose to launch his conducting career with the orchestra when he took it to Spain in 1988. The current principal conductor and artistic adviser is the Finnish conductor and composer Esa-Pekka Salonen.

PIANO

The invention of the piano solved a problem that faced many 18th century keyboard players: the lack of the ability of the clavichord and harpsichord to play loudly and softly. A harpsichord is basically a box of strings which the player plucks via its keys. A clavichord is different because it hits its strings with metal blades called tangents, which stay in position until the keys are released. The volume produced depends on how hard a player can strike the keys.

Either way, there was no sense of light and shade in the playing of both instruments. The man who changed all that was an Italian called Bartolomeo Cristofori. He was born in Padua in 1655 and was possibly a cello or violin maker. While working in Florence for Duke Ferdinand de Medici, he produced a keyboard with an action which used hammers that allowed the strings either to resonate or not, depending on whether the player wanted them to. The hammers then returned to their prone position, ready to be hit again. This gave the new instrument both agility and volume. That unique selling point – the 'nuova inventione che fa'il piano e il forte', as Cristofori put it at the time – led to the instrument gaining the name 'Pianoforte', which translates as 'quiet loud'. Today, this has been shortened simply to 'piano'.

One way of placing the invention of the piano within the history of classical music is to look at the works of Haydn (born 1732) and Mozart (born 1756). That 20-odd year difference meant that Haydn wrote a dozen keyboard concertos whilst Mozart penned twenty seven piano concertos. The latter was one of the first composers to realise the potential of the new pianoforte, writing a stunning body of work which exploited all of its possibilities. Alongside the concertos – Mozart's calling-card showpieces which he frequently used to gain work in a new town or to show what he could do to a new patron – are the 18 piano sonatas, which demonstrate virtually every facet of the instrument.

Mozart's favourite instruments were a Stein piano made in Augsburg and one built by Walter of Vienna, which is on display at the composer's birthplace museum in Salzburg. If you ever see it, you will notice that Mozart had to work with 22 fewer notes than a modern piano. Pianos now have 88 notes, whereas Mozart's Walter had just 66. Pedals were not always pedals, either. The job done by today's 'soft' pedal was often achieved by means of a knob, positioned on the front of the case, which the player would pull with a hand. Intriguingly, a few years before Mozart was born, J.S. Bach was shown the new pianoforte and treated to a demonstration of all it could do, but decided it was not for him.

PREPARED PIANO

This does not refer to a piano which has been tuned and given the once over with furniture polish and vigorous rubbing with a duster. The term 'prepared piano' was coined by the 20th century composer John Cage. In this instance the piano is prepared by having items placed inside the case on the strings. These could range from spoons, to bells, to nuts and bolts. The object is to trigger not only the notes of the piano but a series of extraneous random sounds, too. Cage's *Sonatas and Interludes* are still considered the benchmark in this area.

PIANOLA

Pianolas or 'player pianos' were invented in the 1890s, the Aeolian Company of New York being among the most significant manufacturers of the instrument. Indeed, it is their trade name, Pianola, which has stuck as the word for all player pianos, in much the same way as Hoover became synonymous with vacuum cleaners. Player pianos reproduce both the notes and the expression of a given performance by means of piano rolls. The piano roll is first 'cut' (generally not during an actual performance but by a technician). It can subsequently be 'played' by means of suction pedals, which control not just the speed at which the piece is played but the dynamics as well, making playing a Pianola fairly tricky. Originally intended for homes where no one could play the piano, they have produced a wonderful by-product: rolls 'cut' by famous pianists and even some composers.

POULENC, FRANCIS
1899-1963

Born just before the turn of the 20th century, Francis Jean Marcel Poulenc is as French as his names suggest. His musical education did not follow the normal path; although he did study with various composers, there are whole areas in which he never received any formal instruction. His witty, continental style drew him to ally himself with Satie and the rest of Les Six (a group of six composers all writing in France around the same time). Poulenc rediscovered his Roman Catholicism in the 1930s, resulting in some truly great choral works, such as his *Gloria*. Not surprisingly for a man who once confessed he wished he was Maurice Chevalier, another area in which he made a name was in 'chanson', the French lieder tradition. He created a huge volume of songs, many for his concert partner, Pierre Bernac.

PREMIERE

The French word for 'first' has entered the English language whenever a new musical work is given its debut performance. There have been many notable premieres throughout classical music history, but here are just a couple:

29 May 1913, at the Théâtre des Champs-Élysées

Pierre Monteux conducted, the audience rioted, the police intervened, the composer Saint-Saëns allegedly stormed out in disgust. It was the first performance of Stravinsky's amazing ballet *The Rite of Spring*.

7 May 1824, at the Kärntnortheater, Vienna

In Beethoven's first concert appearance in 12 years, he spent the entire time, on stage, conducting music he could not hear, while another conductor gave the performers the real beat. When the performance of his *Symphony No. 9* ended, Beethoven was still conducting and had to be turned round by the mezzo-soprano soloist, to take the applause.

PROKOFIEV, SERGEI
1891-1953

Prokofiev studied with the composers Glière, Rimsky Korsakov and Liadov. He became enveloped in the Russian Romantic tradition, although he managed to combine this with a natural leaning towards 20th-century modernism. His early works, such as his *Piano Concerto No. 1*, show off his more lyrical side, as does his *Symphony No. 1* (known as the *Classical Symphony*), which was written when he was just 26 years old.

An accomplished concert pianist, Prokofiev left Russia the year after the 1917 Revolution, ostensibly on a recital tour. He stayed out of the country for many years, but in 1936 became one of the few Russian exiles to return home permanently, taking up residence in Moscow. At first, he managed to co-exist with the Soviet authorities. His *Second Violin Concerto* went down well, as did his *Symphony No. 5*. However, his next symphony got him into the Communist Party's bad books; in 1948, together with fellow-composers Shostakovich and Khachaturian, he was denounced by Andrei Zhdanov, Stalin's cultural supremo, for writing music that was considered to be not in the true Soviet spirit.

Aside from his work for the concert hall, Prokofiev became widely respected for his magnificent ballets. *Romeo and Juliet* is the best-known of them, though the Bolshoi, for whom he originally wrote it, declared it impossible to dance. He also composed some striking film scores, notably for Eisenstein's epics, *Alexander Nevsky* and *Ivan the Terrible* as well as a mammoth opera, *War and Peace*. Prokofiev died on 5 March, 1953 – the very same day as Stalin.

† **Recommended Listening:**

Romeo and Juliet

PUCCINI, GIACOMO
1858-1924

Puccini was born into a family that was steeped in music; his father, grandfather and great-grandfather were all musicians. He studied at the Lucca music school and then in Milan at the Conservatoire, where the young Mascagni was a fellow-student.

The future king of Italian opera started off his career at the age of 14 as a church organist. It was only after attending a performance of Verdi's *Aida* four years later that he was bitten by the opera bug.

Inspired by what he had heard, he eventually entered a competition organised by Sonzogno, a leading Italian music publisher of the day, for a new one-act opera. Not only did Puccini's entry, *Le Villi*, fail to win: it was disqualified because the judges said that Puccini's manuscript was illegible. Nevertheless, some of the composer's friends decided they could read the spidery score and organised a staging at a local theatre in Milan. Giulio Ricordi, who had been Verdi's publisher, heard the opera and was impressed enough by it to put its composer on a retainer.

Edgar, the first opera Puccini wrote for Ricordi, was a flop, but *Manon Lescaut*, which followed in 1893, was a smash hit. *La Bohème* (1896), *Tosca* (1900) and *Madam Butterfly* (1904) followed, though the first of these took some time to gain lasting popularity, while the last had to be heavily revised following a disastrous La Scala premiere. Together, they are now regarded as the cornerstones of the operatic repertoire.

There followed a period of silence, probably sparked off by the suicide of Puccini's maid, hounded by rumours of an affair with her boss. He returned to the theatre with *La Fanciulla del West* in 1910, following this with *La Rondine* (1917) and *Il Trittico* (1918), which consists of three one-act operas all performed one after the other. He never finished *Turandot*, his final masterpiece. He was still working on the concluding part of the final act when he died of throat cancer in a Brussels clinic, in 1924.

VERISMO OPERA

Puccini's brand of opera is often labelled as *verismo*, the Italian for realist (from the word *vero*, meaning 'truth'). Such operas concentrate on realistic subject matter – occasionally considered sordid, sometimes scandalous at the time. They also tend to be what is technically termed through-composed, rather than a series of stops and starts for arias and recitatives. As well as Puccini, Mascagni, Leoncavallo, Cilea and Giordano are all considered leading verismo composers.

PURCELL, HENRY
1659-1695

Henry Purcell was born into a long line of musicians in Westminster in 1659. Details of his early life are somewhat sketchy, but he was probably just four years old when his father died and he became a 'child of the Chapel Royal.' As a result, he would almost certainly have been taught by John Blow and Pelham Humphrey – both hugely successful composers in their day.

Purcell remained a member of the Chapel Royal until his voice broke, when he was around 14. Instead of being dismissed – the usual fate of boy choristers who could no longer sing high notes – Purcell was kept on, no doubt because of his other musical talents. He was given a job as Assistant to the Instrument Tuner and spent the next few years looking after the Westminster Abbey organ and copying out music. Eventually, in 1677, he was appointed a court composer. Then, in 1679, he succeeded John Blow as organist of the Abbey itself.

Purcell was a prolific composer. Even by the time he became Westminster Abbey's organist, he had already written a large number of anthems (many with orchestral accompaniment), songs, funeral music, sacred part-songs and music for consorts of viols (the viol was the precursor of the violin). In the 1680s, he premiered *Dido and Aeneas* at Josias Priest's School for Young Ladies in Chelsea (the exact date is uncertain). It is an early landmark in the story of English opera, although Purcell himself referred to it simply as a 'dramatic entertainment.'

Purcell went on to compose four large-scale semi-operatic works in the early 1690s – *King Arthur* is probably the best-known of them – and the incidental music for numerous plays. On his untimely death in 1695, he was buried in Westminster Abbey. His tomb is still there, today, near the organ, alongside the inscription: 'Here lyes Henry Purcell Esq., who left this life and is gone to that blessed place where only his harmony can be exceeded.'

† **Recommended Listening:**

When I am Laid in Earth from *Dido and Aeneas*

R

RACHMANINOV, SERGEI
1873-1943

The last of the great Russian Romantic composers, Rachmaninov was born in Semyonovo, near Novgorod in north-western Russia, into an aristocratic family that was frequently strapped for cash. Eventually, when Rachmaninov was nine years old, the estate on which he had been born had to be sold to pay off his father's debts and the family moved to St. Petersburg, the Russian capital. The teenage boy was already showing signs of musical promise, particularly as a pianist, so it was only natural that he would be enrolled in the St. Petersburg Conservatoire.

Rachmaninov, however, did not get on well with his education, thanks to natural laziness and, in part, problems at home. His much-loved sister died and his father walked out on the family. In the end, he was packed off to Moscow, where he studied piano under Nikolai Zverev, a strict disciplinarian who was one of the few people who could get Rachmaninov to really concentrate on his studies. Nevertheless, despite quarrelling with his teacher about the time he was devoting to composition, he soon started making a name for himself. He began mixing with the likes of Tchaikovsky, Rubinstein and Arensky, spending his summers at Ivanovka, his cousin's country estate, which provided him with the perfect environment for composing.

While still a student, Rachmaninov wrote *Aleko*, a prize-winning one-act opera, the *Piano Concerto No. 1* and *Morceaux de Fantaisie,* a set of piano pieces that included one which was to make the young

Rachmaninov world famous. It was the *Prelude in C sharp minor.*
His publishers, however, let him down. They failed to copyright
the work outside Russia, so they – and Rachmaninov – could only
look on as it was reprinted and reprinted without earning either of
them a rouble.

Things appeared to be going well for Rachmaninov, who was
fast being recognised as a fine pianist and conductor as well as a
promising composer. Part of the reason for his brilliance at the
piano was due to his unusually large hands, with very long fingers
and thumbs. This meant that he could stretch further across the
keyboard than practically any other pianist of the day.

Then disaster struck. The premiere of his *Symphony No. 1* was a
total flop. The conductor (none other than the composer Glazunov)
was said to be drunk and the whole work fell apart in performance.
As a result, Rachmaninov fell into a state of acute depression and
stopped composing altogether. Eventually, Dr. Nikolai Dahl, a noted
amateur musician and a pioneer of psychotherapy, succeeded in
restoring his self-confidence. In gratitude, Rachmaninov dedicated
his *Piano Concerto No. 2* to him. It is probably the composer's best-
loved composition.

The Russian Revolution of 1917 forced Rachmaninov out of his
homeland. Eventually, he settled in the USA – first in New York and
then in Beverley Hills, California – though he continued to tour. He
also built himself a summer villa on the shore of Lake Lucerne in
Switzerland. It became a second Ivanovka – an oasis where he could
compose in peace. His enduringly popular *Rhapsody on a Theme
of Paganini* was among the works that he wrote there. After being
taken ill on a US concert tour, he died of cancer at his Californian
home on 28 March, 1943. He is buried in the Kensico Cemetery,
outside New York.

† **Recommended Listening:**
Piano Concerto No. 2

RAMEAU, JEAN-PHILIPPE
1683-1764

Born in Dijon, Rameau was a contemporary of Handel. A celebrated harpsichordist and organist, he travelled pretty much the length and breadth of France. His fame at the time rested as much on his textbooks about music, as it did on his composing and playing. Once he had settled permanently in Paris from 1722 onwards, he specialised in composing music for the stage. In his fifties, he rapidly inherited from Lully the position of being the most respected name in French opera. His pioneering work brought him to the attention of, first, the superbly-named financier, Alexandre le Riche de la Poupeliniere (for whom he worked) and subsequently Louis XV himself. For the last two decades of his life he was the Royal Chamber Music Composer.

† **Recommended Listening:**

Overture to the ballet-opera *Les Indes Galantes*

RATTLE, SIR SIMON
1955-

Born in Liverpool, Simon Rattle was very talented very young, rising through the Merseyside Youth Orchestra and then the National Youth Orchestra. He played the piano, violin and percussion, but it was conducting that always attracted him. He studied it at London's Royal Academy of Music from the age of 16 and, three years later won the John Player International Conducting Competition. The prize was a two-year assistant conductorship with the Bournemouth Symphony Orchestra.

After successes with the Nash Ensemble, the Philharmonia Orchestra (at the record-breaking age of 21) and the Royal Liverpool Philharmonic Orchestra, Rattle became Music Director of the City of Birmingham Symphony Orchestra in 1980. He was to remain with the orchestra for 18 years. Under him, the CBSO won an international reputation; it soon became clear that Rattle was a conductor of genius as he worked wonder after wonder with his band. His spectacular 'Towards the Millennium' series of concerts – and, indeed, the CBSO's move into the new Symphony Hall in 1991 – were highlights of his period with the orchestra.

In 2002, Rattle succeeded Claudio Abbado as Chief Conductor of the Berlin Philharmonic, possibly the greatest orchestra in the world. After an initially stormy honeymoon, he took the orchestra to even greater heights of accomplishment, with the result that his contract with it has been extended to 2020.

RAVEL, MAURICE
1875-1937

French composer Maurice Ravel studied composition with Fauré, trying three times to win the Prix de Rome, the most prestigious prize offered by the Paris Conservatoire. His lack of success became something of a scandal; his music was considered too radical by the conservatives who judged the competition.

At around the same time as he was battling with the Conservatoire authorities, Ravel joined an avant-garde group of writers, artists and musicians, known as the 'Apaches'. He became something of a dandy, with a penchant for showy ties and frilly shirts. Musically, it was a productive period for him. He produced a succession of great works, such as the opera *L'Heure Espagnole*, *Valse Nobles et Sentimentales*, which he composed for the piano but later rescored for orchestra, and the ballet *Daphnis et Chloé*, which he wrote for Serge Diaghilev's Ballets Russes. It was through this commission that Ravel met Stravinsky, who became a firm friend. His relationship with Debussy, however, deteriorated over time. Maybe the older composer took offence at Ravel's reported remark that, if he had the time, he 'would re-orchestrate *La Mer*'.

When the First World War broke out, Ravel tried to get into the army, but was turned down because of his ill-health. Later, he volunteered to serve as an ambulance driver on the front near Verdun, but was discharged in 1917, suffering from fever, exhaustion and insomnia. After the war, he composed less, though he still produced exceptional works, such as *La Valse* and *Boléro*. Though it became his best-known composition, he came to dislike the latter work, describing it as 'a piece for orchestra without music'. He died after a long illness in 1937.

† **Recommended Listening:**
Piano Concerto in D for Left Hand

REGER, MAX
1873-1916

Among the very few composers with a palindrome for a name, Reger was born in Bavaria. As well as being a composer, he was a virtuoso organist, whose performances did much to rekindle popularity for the instrument. He also had a passion for the music of Bach and Beethoven. Having settled in Munich at the age of 28, Reger won fame as a solo performer and as an accompanist, before moving to take up the post of Director of Music at the University of Leipzig. A heavy drinker, he died from a heart attack, aged only 43. He is remembered for his mordant wit as well as for his music. He famously responded to a critic: 'I am sitting in the smallest room of my house. I have your review in front of me. Very shortly, it will be behind me'.

† **Recommended Listening:**
Cello Suite No. 1

Requiem

Strictly speaking, a Requiem is a Roman Catholic mass for the dead, containing the following sections: *Requiem Aeternam*, *Dies Irae*, *Domine Jesu Christe*, *Sanctus*, *Agnus Dei*, *Lux Aeterna* and finally the *Libera Me*. However, many composers down the centuries have added extra liturgical sections and also used secular words. Fauré added the *In Paradisum* to his *Requiem*, for example, while Howard Goodall featured English poetry in his *Eternal Light*. Other well-known requiems include those by Mozart, Duruflé, Berlioz, Verdi, Rutter, Jenkins and Britten.

Respighi, Ottorino
1879-1936
Respighi studied first in his hometown of Bologna, becoming a proficient violinist, before taking lessons in composition in Russia with Rimksy-Korsakov, and, briefly, in Berlin with Bruch. As well as playing in a string quintet, he became the Director of the Academy of St. Cecilia in Rome before giving up the position to allow himself more time to compose. He is best remembered today for his orchestral 'pictures' – studies such as the *Fountains of Rome* and the *Pines of Rome*, as well as *The Birds*, which replicates authentic bird-calls. Respighi was much admired by Mussolini, though he claimed not to reciprocate the Italian dictator's feelings.
† **Recommended Listening:**
  Pines of Rome

Rimsky-Korsakov, Nikolai
1844-1908
A hugely influential Russian composer, orchestrator and teacher (of, amongst others, Stravinsky), Rimsky-Korsakov came from a rich, aristocratic family. Like generations of his family before him, he wanted

to be a sailor, becoming a naval cadet at the age of 12. He took time out for piano lessons along the way and it was his piano teacher who introduced him to the composer Balakirev. He then met Cui, Mussorgsky and Borodin (the group known as 'The Five' or 'The Mighty Handful').

It was Balakirev, in particular, who inspired Rimsky-Korsakov to take up composition seriously. While still serving in the navy, he was made Professor of Composition and Orchestration at the St. Petersburg Conservatoire at the spectacularly early age of 27. Later, he was able to combine his two passions when he became Inspector of Naval Bands, a post specially created for him by the Russian Admiralty.

Hearing Wagner's *Ring cycle* for the first time in 1889 when a touring German opera company brought it to St. Petersburg, was a turning point in the 44-year-old composer's life. From then on, he devoted most of his time to composing for the stage himself. In all, he wrote 15 operas, of which *The Tale of Tsar Saltan* (1900, from which comes *The Flight of the Bumble Bee*) and *The Golden Cockerel* (1907) are the best-known examples. As well as being a fine composer in his own right, he was a keen completer and orchestrator of other people's music, as his work on Mussorgsky's *Boris Godunov* and Borodin's *Prince Igor* testifies.

† **Recommended Listening:**

The Young Prince and the Young Princess
from the symphonic suite *Scheherazade.*

RODRIGO, JOAQUÍN

1902-1999

The most Spanish of composers, Rodrigo was born not far from Valencia. After contracting diphtheria he lost most of his eyesight at the age of three, but this did not put a stop to his musical progress. He studied in Valencia, then with Paul Dukas in Paris, writing all his compositions in Braille. He returned to Spain in 1939, the same year in which he wrote his *Concierto De Aranjuez*. Inspired by the beautiful palace at Aranjuez, this guitar concerto is probably his best-known work, though, curiously enough, Rodrigo himself never mastered the playing of the instrument. In his forties, Rodrigo became Director of Music at the University of Madrid. There, he put himself at the head of the casticismo (authenticity) movement, which aimed to revive Spanish music by going back to its folk traditions and rediscovering its lost Baroque customs. He was widely travelled, giving lectures and piano recitals, and being honoured by virtually every European country. He was Spain's most enduring musical celebrity of the latter half of the 20th century.

† **Recommended Listening:**
   Fantasia para un gentilhombre

Romantic Period

Even the actual dates of the Romantic period in classical music are frequently disputed, so it is easy to see how a precise definition of the term might be tricky to establish. Romantic music has been claimed to cover any piece of music written from 1815 (some say as late as 1830) onwards to 1900 or 1910, although, as shown in our list of ten favourites opposite, some composers continued to write romantic music well beyond the 1930s.

   As a definable term, it is possible to get to grips with it only by means of placing it in the context of other musical periods. This way, it can be seen as simply the maturing of the Classical period, which was itself a maturing of – and occasionally a reaction to – the Baroque period. If we accept the argument that the rules of music had been worked out in the Baroque period and then explored in the Classical one, they undoubtedly were now stretched to their limit and broken. As part of a movement which saw the same happening in art and literature – particularly between 1830 and 1850 – Romantic composers shook off the shackles in favour of free-ranging expression. Music was allowed to paint pictures, to evoke poems and to play on the emotions.

TEN FAVOURITE ROMANTIC WORKS:

1 Rachmaninov: *Piano Concerto No. 2* Composed in 1901/2, Rachmaninov's enduring work shows that no matter how late you enter the Romantic fray, you can see off the competition with one of the most 'romantic' tunes ever written.

2 Beethoven: *Piano Concerto No. 5 ('The Emperor')* Many people consider Beethoven's early works as being from the Classical period and his later works as epitomising the Romantic one. This is one of his earlier Romantic works (composed between 1809 and 1811); it has a powerful solo piano introduction.

3 Bruch: *Violin Concerto No. 1* Right at the heart of the Romantic era, Bruch worked and reworked this concerto until he got it exactly as he wanted it – with a little help from the great violinist Joseph Joachim, who premiered the work.

4 Beethoven: *Symphony No. 9* Quite possibly the epitome of the Romantic symphony, it was finished in 1824 but influenced composers for decades.

5 Elgar: *Variations on an Original Theme* (known as *The Enigma Variations*) Elgar's collection of tributes to his friends was a hit when it premiered in 1899, with Glazunov, Rimsky-Korsakov and Mahler as early champions.

6 Grieg: *Piano Concerto* It could be argued that there is no more Romantic an opening to any work than the piano 'storm' that is released at the outset of this amazing piece.

7 Saint-Saëns: *Symphony No. 3 ('The Organ')* Thanks to a commission from the Royal Philharmonic Society, London audiences were the first to hear this fabulous Romantic colossus.

8 Tchaikovsky: *1812 Overture* The gigantic proportions of this mighty work must have rocked the foundations of the recently built Church of Christ the Saviour in Moscow, where it was premiered.

9 Rachmaninov: *Symphony No. 2* Rachmaninov continued the Romantic style of composition almost single-handedly well into the 20th century. The third movement of this work is among the finest examples of Romantic sound.

10 Beethoven: *Symphony No. 7* The premiere of this work in 1813 must have been quite something, with its all-star orchestra: Hummel, Spohr, Meyerbeer and Salieri were all in the band, with Beethoven himself conducting.

ROSSINI, GIOACHINO
1792-1868

Believe it or not, his parents originally intended Rossini to become a blacksmith, despite having a singer for a mother and a wayward horn-player as a father. At the age of 14, however, he was enrolled in the Music Academy in Bologna; four years later, he wrote his first full-scale opera, one of the staggering total of 39 he composed during his career. Though he wrote sacred and chamber music as well, it is as a masterful operatic composer that he is best known.

Once Rossini had started, he could not stop. Year after year, the operas poured from his pen. Initially, *Tancredi*, a tragedy based on a play by Voltaire, and the sparkling comedy *The Italian Girl in Algiers* were his greatest successes. By the time he was 23, he had signed a contract to produce two operas a year, one for each of the two opera houses in Naples. It was for Rome, however, that he created *The Barber of Seville*, perhaps his greatest comic opera of all.

Rossini married the soprano Isabella Colbran when he was 30, after which he began to travel more. He met Beethoven in Vienna – according to Rossini, the German composer made disparaging comments about Italians – and visited Britain. He settled, though, in Paris, where he composed *William Tell*, his grandest and longest operatic work. By now, he had made so much money out of opera that he wrote nothing more for the stage. After returning home to Italy for a while, he eventually went back to the French capital, where he devoted the rest of his life to fine living and dining.

† **Recommended Listening:**
  Overture to *William Tell*

ROYAL LIVERPOOL PHILHARMONIC ORCHESTRA

It might seem surprising to some that Liverpool is the home of the country's oldest surviving symphony orchestra. The 'Phil' (as it is universally known on Merseyside) can trace its origins back to 1840. It became a fully professional band in 1853, five years before the UK's next oldest symphony orchestra – the Hallé down the road in Manchester.

The orchestra was founded by some well-to-do merchants, who wanted to ensure that Liverpool's cultural life rivalled that of the capital. They built their own Philharmonic Hall on Hope Street in 1849. It was destroyed by fire in 1933 with a brand new replacement opening in 1939. It is still the orchestra's home. Over the years, the list of its Principal Conductors has included Sir Malcolm Sargent, Sir John Pritchard, Sir Charles Groves and, in more recent times, the eminent Czech conductor Libor Pešek.

The RLPO has been a prolific recording orchestra. In the days of 78s, there were famous versions of *Messiah* and *The Dream of Gerontius*, both conducted by Sargent. Later, it made pioneering first recordings of English works – notably by Delius and Bax – under the batons of Groves and Vernon Handley. It made a notable cycle of the Beethoven symphonies, conducted by Sir Charles Mackerras, and is recording all the Shostakovich symphonies, directed by the dynamic young Russian Vasily Petrenko, who is the orchestra's current chief conductor.

ROYAL OPERA HOUSE

The original Theatre Royal, Covent Garden (the name comes from its historical convent garden site) was built by actor-manager John Rich out of the fortune he made, aptly enough, from his staging of *The Beggar's Opera*. Many of Handel's great operas were premiered there, but, in 1808, the theatre was gutted by fire, with 23 firemen losing their lives as the building collapsed in the blaze. The replacement theatre opened just over a year later; in 1847, it became the Royal Italian Opera.

Then, disaster struck again. In 1856, the theatre was destroyed by fire for the second time. The third and present theatre opened two years later; in 1892, it was renamed the Royal Opera House. Up until 1914, it staged spectacular summer opera seasons, but, during the First World War, it served as a furniture store. Opera returned in 1919, but, in 1939, it became a dance hall. Extensively redeveloped in the 1990s, it has been the home of both the Royal Opera and the Royal Ballet since 1946.

ROYAL OPERA
Granted its royal title in 1968 (before then, it had been the Covent Garden Opera Company), the Royal Opera performs works in their original language with guest artists singing most major roles (in contrast to English National Opera, which sings in English with a company of contracted singers). The Orchestra of the Royal Opera House is the resident band, playing for both opera and ballet.

ROYAL BALLET
Founded in 1931 by Dame Ninette de Valois (it began life as the Academy of Choreographic Art before becoming the Sadler's Wells Ballet), the Royal Ballet moved into Covent Garden in 1946, gaining its royal status in 1956.

ROYAL PHILHARMONIC ORCHESTRA
Founded in 1946 by the flamboyant conductor Sir Thomas Beecham, the Royal Philharmonic Orchestra is based in London at Chelsea's Cadogan Hall, though it also gives regular performances at the Royal Albert Hall and at the Royal Festival Hall. The orchestra's debut performance was at the Davis Theatre in Croydon and it has continued to perform in the town ever since. The RPO also visits Northampton, Crawley, Lowestoft and Reading on a regular basis.

Beecham made the orchestra one of the world's great bands. After his death in 1961, which the orchestra managed to survive, it turned to other notable conductors, including Rudolf Kempe, André Previn, Antal Dorati, Walter Weller and Daniele Gatti. The current Artistic Director is Charles Dutoit. The RPO has enjoyed a long partnership with the concert promoter Raymond Gubbay, often featuring at his Classical Spectacular concerts. It has recorded extensively and streams its entire Cadogan Hall concert series over the internet.

ROYAL PHILHARMONIC SOCIETY

The Royal Philharmonic Society was founded in London in 1813 by a group of wealthy music-lovers, its aim being 'to promote the performance, in the most perfect manner possible of the best and most approved instrumental music'. Among the many famous works composed as a result of a commission from the society, Beethoven's *Symphony No. 9* must rank as the greatest. During its long history, the Society has also commissioned music from Mendelssohn, Dvošák, Vaughan Williams and Elgar. Today, the RPS continues to support contemporary composers, as well as working to provide young musicians with a concert platform and generally promoting a greater appreciation of classical music.

ROYAL SCOTTISH NATIONAL ORCHESTRA

Originally known simply as 'The Scottish Orchestra', the Royal Scottish National Orchestra was founded in 1891. Over the years, it has been conducted by an impressive list of great musicians, not least Sir John Barbirolli and George Szell, but, aptly enough, it was thanks to the leadership of Scottish-born Sir Alexander Gibson that the orchestra really flowered to win international renown.

From 1959, Gibson conducted the orchestra for 25 years, becoming the longest-serving Music Director in the orchestra's history. Under him, the orchestra became famous for its performances of Scandinavian music, notably that of Sibelius and Carl Nielsen. Gibson also took the orchestra into the pit when he founded Scottish Opera. In 1991, the orchestra was granted permission to add the 'Royal' to its title (it had been renamed the Scottish National Orchestra in 1950).

Today, under its talented French Music Director Stéphane Denève, the RSNO's home is still Glasgow, though it also performs in Edinburgh, Dundee, Aberdeen, Perth and Inverness. Its recording reputation is particularly impressive with eight Grammy nominations between 2002 and 2009 alone. A project to record all eight Glazunov symphonies with José Serebrier continues, as does a complete cycle of the music of French composer Roussel, with Denève conducting. The first disc in this series won the prestigious Diapason d'Or de l'Annèe for Symphonic Music.

RUTTER, JOHN
1945-

Known chiefly for his choral music, composer and conductor John Rutter studied at Clare College, Cambridge, in the 1960s, returning there in 1975 as Director of Music. He left four years later and went on to form his own Cambridge Singers, a group dedicated to performing and recording, amongst other works, his own extensive body of compositions.

Rutter is probably the most widely-performed English composer of his generation. He is particularly noted for his Christmas carols, though he has also composed various anthems and, on a grander scale, a notable *Gloria*, *Magnificat* and a *Requiem*. There is a strong following for his music among amateur choirs, particularly in the USA. Favourite Rutter works include *A Gaelic Blessing*, which was commissioned by a choir in Nebraska, and *For the Beauty of the Earth*, a resetting of the old hymn.

† **Recommended Listening:**
  Requiem, Candlelight Carol

S

Saint Louis Symphony Orchestra

The Saint Louis Symphony is the second oldest American symphony orchestra (the oldest is the New York Philharmonic). It was founded in 1880 by Dutch-born choir conductor Joseph Otten with just 31 musicians. Based in the (allegedly haunted) Powell Symphony Hall, today it is led by American-born music director David Robertson, who has taken the orchestra to critical heights. Other noted conductors to have stood on the podium include Itzhak Perlman and Leonard Slatkin. It was Slatkin's long musical directorship, from 1979 to 1996, that saw a real growth in the SLSO's musical prestige. There were problems, though. In 2001, the orchestra nearly went bankrupt, while, in 2005, the musicians staged a two-month strike.

St. Petersburg Philharmonic Orchestra

Russia's oldest symphony orchestra was founded in 1882, originally as the private court orchestra of Tsar Alexander III. Following the Russian Revolution in 1917, it became the State Philharmonic Orchestra of Petrograd before being named the Leningrad Philharmonic Orchestra three years later. It reverted to its original name in 1991.

The St. Petersburg Philharmonic is generally regarded as one of the world's greatest orchestras, thanks in the main to conductor Evgeny Mravinsky, who was its Music Director for an amazing 50 years from 1938 to 1988. Illustrious guest conductors included Otto Klemperer, Felix Weingartner and Bruno Walter. Prokofiev premiered his piano concertos with the orchestra; it also gave the first performances of eight of Shostakovich's 15 symphonies. The current Chief Conductor is Yuri Temirkanov.

SAINT-SAËNS, CAMILLE
1835-1921

French composer Camille Saint-Saëns was an early developer. He gave his first piano recital when he was aged only nine and entered the Paris Conservatoire just two years later. There, his dazzling talents won him the admiration of Gounod, Rossini, Berlioz and Liszt. When his Symphony No.1 was premiered, Berlioz quipped 'He knows everything but lacks... inexperience!' For his part, Liszt hailed his lifelong friend as the finest organist in the world.

As a church organist, Saint-Saëns started off at a small church on the Rue Saint Martin, before moving in 1857 to the prestigious La Madeleine, where he remained until 1875. For some of the time, he also taught piano, the young Fauré being his favourite pupil. Later, he was instrumental in the founding of the Société Nationale de Musique, an association for the promotion of new French music.

Composing was always Saint-Saëns' first love. As well as his symphonies – the *Third*, the so-called *Organ Symphony*, is a real Romantic monster of a work – he turned out symphonic poems, concertos, chamber music, church music and 13 operas, though only one of these, *Samson and Delilah*, is much performed today. His best-known composition, though, is probably *The Carnival of the Animals*. At least in its composer's lifetime, it had a chequered career. Concerned that the piece – a suite with 14 short movements, each describing a particular animal – was too frivolous and so likely to damage his reputation as a serious composer, Saint-Saëns forbade its public performance. He only allowed one movement of it, *The Swan*, to be published while he was still alive.

In old age, Saint-Saëns found himself falling out of musical favour. Though he had started off as a radical composer, he hated the music of his younger contemporaries – notably that of Debussy – which he failed to understand. Accordingly, he spent much of his time travelling, spending his last years in Algiers, where he died from pneumonia in 1921. He is buried in the Montparnasse Cemetery, Paris, along with Chabrier, Auric and César Franck.

† **Recommended Listening:**

The Carnival of the Animals

SALIERI, ANTONIO
1750-1825

An Italian composer and conductor from Legnano, near Milan, Antonio Salieri originally studied singing in Venice. When he was 16, he moved, with the help of the Bohemian composer, Florian Leopold Gassmann, to Vienna. He worked there, chiefly producing operas, until he was 28 at which point he returned to Italy. In his mid-thirties, he moved to take over from Gluck at the Paris opera, before returning to Vienna, where he became Court Conductor from 1788 until the year before his death. Despite being considered Mozart's rival and arch-enemy – the two were certainly competing for commissions in the opera market place – Salieri almost certainly did not have him poisoned, despite the popular myth that holds that he did.

† **Recommended Listening:**

The Salieri Album (Cecilia Bartoli)

SATIE, ERIK
1866-1925

Born in Honfleur, Satie spent his early years being shunted between there and Paris, where his parents had moved when he was six years old. After an unsuccessful spell at the Paris Conservatoire – 'a local penitentiary' as he put it – he became a cabaret pianist at Montmartre's famous 'Chat Noir'. It was around this time he wrote his *Gymnopédies*, a set of three piano pieces that are probably his best-known work. In his 30s he wrote little, but, following lessons at the Schola Cantorum (a private music school established in 1896 which Albeniz and, later, Messiaen also attended), the now 50-something composer set out on a new and somewhat eccentric path. He grew into something of a cult figure; titles such as *Sketches and Provocative Gestures of a Big Wooden Fellow* and *Drivelling Preludes (for a Dog)* helped. In 1917, he wrote *Parade*, a ballet for Diaghilev for which Jean Cocteau provided the story, after which he became associated with the Surrealist and Dadaist art movements. He died, from cirrhosis of the liver, brought about through years of heavy drinking, in 1925.

† **Recommended Listening:**

  Gymnopédies

SAXOPHONE

Despite being born and raised in Belgium, Adolphe Sax was in his late twenties and living in Paris when he invented his saxophone in the 1840s. Like a clarinet, it is a wind instrument with a single-reed mouthpiece. However, unlike a clarinet, it has a fairly simple fingering system. It has a 'conical bore' (it is wider at the bottom than it is at the top) and is very popular in military bands, not to mention jazz groups.

The Russian composer Glazunov loved the sound the saxophone produced and wrote his *Concerto for Alto Saxophone and Strings* in 1934 after repeated requests from Sigurd Rascher, a legendary Swedish saxophonist. The combination of medieval plainchant and improvised jazz brought together by the saxophonist Jan Garbarek and the Hilliard Ensemble, a noted early music group, for the album *Officium* in 1993 is an enduring Classic FM favourite.

SCARLATTI, DOMENICO
1685-1757

The son of composing father Alessandro, Domenico Scarlatti was born in Naples in the same year as Handel and Bach. As well as being a composer himself, he was an outstanding harpsichordist who, according to legend, 'fought' Handel in a keyboard duel (adjudged to be a draw). Early on, he worked mainly in Rome before spending nine years in Lisbon, composing for Princess Maria Barbara. Eventually, he followed her to Madrid (she married into the Spanish royal family and eventually became Queen of Spain), where he remained until he died. While in Spain, he composed an amazing 555 keyboard sonatas, which paved the way for the later sonatas of Mozart and Beethoven.

† **Recommended Listening:**
Sonata in E Major K 531

SCHERZO

The Italian word for joke has given its name to a lively musical work, or a movement of a work (often a symphony). Developed from the 'minuet and trio', it is usually light in style, and sometimes a little fast and furious. Beethoven was one of the first to grab the scherzo by the scruff of the neck and make it his own. In the third movement of his *Pastoral Symphony*, he used the trappings of the scherzo to depict 'peasants' merrymaking', complete with dancing and the sound of a country band.

In the scherzo from his incidental music for *A Midsummer Night's Dream*, Mendelssohn took advantage of the jokey nature of the movement to represent the character Puck, who was known for his fondness for pranks.

Schubert, Franz
1797-1828

Schubert's father was a schoolteacher in Vienna, who taught the youngster the basic rudiments of music. After being spotted by the eminent composer Salieri when he was only seven, Schubert was enrolled into the Stadtkonvikt (the imperial boarding school) as a boy soprano. He also played violin in the school orchestra, while Salieri himself taught him musical theory and the principles of composition.

The family was always short of money, so, when Schubert left the Stadtkonvikt, he was forced to combine his musical activities with teaching in his father's school. This did not stop him composing. By 1814, he had already produced some piano pieces, songs, some string quartets, his first symphony and a three-act opera. The following year, he wrote *Gretchen am Spinnrade* (*Gretchen at the spinning-wheel*), *Der Erlkonig* (*The Earl King*) and many other great songs, plus two more symphonies, three masses and four stage works.

It was a remarkable display of creativity by any standards. 'I compose every morning', Schubert once said, 'and when one piece is done, I begin another'. Aged 20, he gave up teaching in order to compose full time. At first, things went well for him. He produced more overtures, symphonies, theatre music, chamber music and songs and his works began to be performed in public. Then, he suffered some major setbacks. Strained friendships, financial pressures and serious illness – in 1822, he almost certainly contracted the syphilis that eventually killed him – were the causes. Nevertheless, he soldiered on composing. In his last two years alone, he produced an unparalleled profusion of wonderful music, including *Die Winterreise* (*The Winter Journey*), his last and most amazing song cycle.

† **Recommended Listening:**
 Trout Quintet

SCHUMANN, ROBERT
1810-1856

Robert Schumann was born in Zwickau, some 50 miles south of Leipzig and not far from the Czech border. He started studying the piano at the age of seven, entering the Zwickau Gymnasium four years later. Once in school, his bookish nature blossomed alongside his musical one; he eventually went on to study law at Leipzig and Heidelberg universities.

Schumann began taking piano lessons from Friedrich Wieck when he was 19, having met his teacher's daughter the year before. His plans to become a concert pianist suffered a setback when, at the age of 22, he began to suffer from problems with his right hand, probably a symptom of mercury poisoning (he was being treated with the chemical to combat syphilis). By now, though, he was emerging as a music critic of note.

At the same time, Schumann was pursuing the hand of Clara Wieck, totally against the wishes of her father. Determined not to be beaten, Schumann went to court to fight Wieck's objections to the marriage, but, in the end, the couple had to wait until she was old enough to marry without her father's consent. They were blissfully happy together, a state of mind reflected in the wonderful compositions Schumann was now producing. They included many glorious songs and piano pieces, followed by symphonies, other chamber music and some choral works.

When he reached 33, Schumann started teaching at the conservatory Mendelssohn had founded in Leipzig, though he found time to journey with his wife on a concert tour of Russia (in one instance being asked by a concert goer 'Are you a musician, too?'). Soon after this, Schumann suffered his first bout of severe depression. These attacks were to become more serious as time went by until, when he was 44, he tried to drown himself by jumping off a bridge into the River Rhine. Upon being rescued by some passing boatmen, he asked to be taken to an asylum. He remained there for two years until his death.

† **Recommended Listening:**
  Piano Concerto in A Minor

CLARA SCHUMANN

Clara Schumann must have been a formidable woman. She resolutely fought her father when it came to her marriage to Robert, and stuck by him until his sad end. At this point, she became the chief interpreter of his music, bringing it to as wide an audience as possible, while holding his memory dear enough to stave off the advances of Schumann's last protégé, the young Brahms.

After her husband died, in 1856, Clara continued to tour for more than 30 years. She also found time to be head of piano studies at the conservatoire in Frankfurt, as well as, eventually, caring for a number of her grandchildren and her children (tragically, her son Ludwig ended his days insane like his father). Her own compositions have become increasingly popular in recent years, a fitting turnaround for someone whose music played second fiddle to that of her husband during her lifetime.

SCORE

A score is a printed or handwritten copy of a piece of music, which shows all the parts necessary for a complete performance, arranged on different staves. A full orchestral score is a mass of around 30 or so separate lines, each allowing the conductor to see the music played by a certain instrument or group of instruments of the orchestra.

Scores often come in reduced formats, one of the most common being a piano score, where the full orchestral part has been reduced down to be playable by a pianist, a task often undertaken by the composer himself.

SCOTTISH CHAMBER ORCHESTRA

A relative newcomer in musical circles, the Scottish Chamber Orchestra was founded in 1974. It performs throughout Scotland, touring the Highlands and Islands as well as the southern part of the country each year. Further commitments to the Edinburgh, East Neuk and St. Magnus

Festivals have ensured that it is heard by a wide fan base. Conductors have included Jukka-Pekka Saraste and its Conductor Laureate, Sir Charles Mackerras. The orchestra's present principal conductor is London-born Robin Ticciati.

SCOTTISH OPERA

Founded in 1962 by the conductor Sir Alexander Gibson, Scottish Opera originally presented seasons in Edinburgh and Aberdeen (even travelling as far afield as Newcastle). The company moved into the newly refurbished Theatre Royal, Glasgow, in 1975. In 1980, the Orchestra of Scottish Opera was founded. Having achieved notable successes with premieres, such as Ines de Castro by James McMillan, it continues to champion the widest range of opera, of the highest standard, in front of the largest possible audience right across Scotland.

SCRIABIN, ALEXANDER
1872-1915

Born in Moscow, Scriabin was the son of a lawyer and a pianist. Unsurprisingly, he excelled in piano from a young age and, despite being enrolled at military cadet school in early boyhood, managed to keep up his playing. When he was 16, he switched to studying music at the Moscow Conservatoire, tackling composition with the composer Arensky as well as continuing his piano studies. A publishing deal he made while still at college allowed him to tour his own works when he was just 24.

Scriabin became piano professor at his old conservatoire aged 26, but gave it up to settle in Switzerland in 1903. He was increasingly attracted to theosophy and other mystical philosophies, composing his works from this time onwards as heralds, so he said, of a forthcoming disaster. He also had synaesthesia – that is, he 'saw' musical keys in colour.

Accordingly, he designed what he called a 'clavier à lumières' – a colour organ – to feature in his massive symphonic work *Poem of Fire.* Instead of sounds, it projected colours when played.

† **Recommended Listening:**
  Etude in D sharp minor Op. 8 No.12

SHOSTAKOVICH, DMITRI
1906-1975

After Stravinsky, Shostakovich was the foremost Russian composer of the 20th century. First taught by his mother, he attended what was then the Petrograd Conservatoire, aged only 13, completing the course in just four years. His *Symphony No. 1*, which he completed when he was aged only 20, made him a musical celebrity and his reputation grew over the years. He was one of the first composers to write substantially for film as well as for the concert hall and the stage.

It was opera, though, that was to prove Shostakovich's undoing. In 1930, *The Nose* was condemned by the Communist regime for its 'bourgeois decadence' and he had to withdraw it. His next stage work, *Lady Macbeth of Mtsensk*, which was premiered in 1936, fared no better. In an attack probably inspired by Stalin himself, *Pravda*, the official Communist newspaper, denounced him for producing 'chaos instead of music'. The following year, Shostakovich's response was to write his *Symphony No. 5*, which he subtitled 'a Soviet artist's creative reply to just criticism'. It swiftly became one of his most popular works, as did his *Symphony No. 7*, which he wrote while besieged in Leningrad during the Second World War.

The reprieve was short lived, however. In 1948, he was denounced as 'anti-people' and relieved of his professorship – a post he only regained 12 years later. Stalin's death in 1953, and the ensuing period of slightly freer thinking, saw the appearance of his tour de force, his *Symphony No. 10*, a piece which uses his initials as a recurring motto. From then onwards, his reputation started to grow again. By the time of his death, he had written a full 15 symphonies.

† **Recommended Listening:**

Romance from *The Gadfly*

SIBELIUS, JEAN

1865-1957

Alongside the piano, Sibelius's first love was violin. He longed to be a concert violinist, although he also studied composition from books. When he was 20, he started studying law at Helsinki University, but soon switched both venues and subject, enrolling to study music at the city's conservatoire a year later.

Gradually, composition became the dominant factor in Sibelius's musical life. He took lessons in Berlin and Vienna, before returning to teach in Helsinki. When he was 27, he composed *En Saga*, a tone poem, and *Kullervo*, a nationalist choral symphony. Just five years later, the Finnish state awarded him an annual pension to allow him to do nothing but compose. Two years after that, the government's faith in him paid off when he wrote another tone poem, this time called *Finlandia*. It was to become the country's unofficial national anthem.

The composition of *Finlandia* also coincided, more or less, with Sibelius's first foray into symphonies, which, from then on, were to form the backbone of his musical output. He consoled the violinist inside himself by writing a *Violin Concerto* when he was 38. He wrote his *Symphony No. 5* during the First World War. By 1924, he had completed seven symphonies (he later completed and destroyed an eighth). Much like Rossini, he practically stopped composing for the last 26 years of his life, resting on the laurels of the legendary status he had gained in his homeland; Sibelius stamps were even issued in his honour.

† **Recommended Listening:**

Finlandia

SINGERS
Singers divide into six main categories:

SOPRANO AND MEZZO SOPRANOS
The highest of the female registers is called a soprano (a treble, if it is a boy). In the 17th and 18th centuries, the male soprano would have been a castrato. Mezzo sopranos (meaning literally 'half' sopranos) sing between the soprano and alto ranges. Famous sopranos include: Joan Sutherland, Renée Fleming, Emma Kirkby, Lesley Garrett, Lucia Popp and Dawn Upshaw. Famous mezzo sopranos include: Janet Baker, Christa Ludwig and Magdalena Kožená.

ALTO
The word means 'high', which is a little confusing considering they are the lower of the two main female registers (this is because, originally, all parts were sung by men and alto itself was short for contratenor altus, shortened to contralto and then alto). Famous altos include: Clara Butt, Kathleen Ferrier and Marian Anderson.

TENOR
If the origins of the alto and baritone names are misleading, then the tenor is downright bizarre. It means 'holding' – nothing to do with register, but all to do with its role in medieval times when the tenors sang a 'holding' tune, around which others sang counterpoints. Nowadays, tenors are very much the leading men of the opera world, almost always the heroes. Famous tenors include: Luciano Pavarotti, José Carreras, Plácido Domingo, Jussi Björling, José Cura and Ian Bostridge.

BARITONE
The word comes from the Greek barytonos, meaning deep sounding, though, in actuality, baritones do not sing as low as all that. Fauré's *Requiem* contains a beautiful part for solo baritone. Famous baritones

include: Dietrich Fischer-Dieskau, Sir Geraint Evans, Sherrill Milnes, Bryn Terfel and Sir Thomas Allen.

Bass

The lowest of the male voices, very often basses are the villains or, perhaps because of their grand nature, the kings in opera. Famous basses include: Boris Christoff, Gottlob Frick, Ruggiero Raimondi, Samuel Ramey and Paata Burchuladze.

A SINGER'S GLOSSARY

Bel Canto: literally beautiful singing, often used to refer to the type of role written by such composers as Bellini, where beauty is rated higher than dramatic punch.

Counter Tenor: the alto register as sung by a man.

Descant: from a mixture of different derivations, today descant means the improvised-sounding higher tune added to the last verse of a hymn or carol.

Perfect Pitch: the ability to sing any named note, without recourse to instrumental help. Leonard Bernstein, André Previn, Yo-Yo Ma and Mozart all have/had it.

Recital: a concert by a soloist or small number of artists (as opposed to, say, a symphony orchestra concert).

Shanty: a song originally sung at sea, using only voices, during hard physical work.

SMETANA, BEDŘICH
1824-1884

Smetana is generally recognised as being the father of Czech music, with his art and fortunes closely tied to his country's struggle for independence; he manned the barricades during the failed nationalist uprising in 1848. Having played piano in public from an early age, he went, via teaching and conducting, into a life as a concert pianist, in order to pay the bills. It was only much later, after doing a job as music critic in Prague, that he finally gained public acclaim, aged 42.

Later, Smetana started to suffer from increasing deafness. He took refuge in the country, where he composed his influential set of musical portraits of his native land, which he titled *Má Vlást* ('*My Fatherland*'). He eventually fell victim to mental health problems and died, aged 60, in an asylum.

† **Recommended Listening:**
  Vltava (The Moldau) from *Má Vlást*

SOLTI, GEORG
1912-1997

Born Gyorgy Stern in Budapest, Georg Solti was taught by the best: Bartók and Dohnányi were his piano teachers and Kodály his composition tutor. In the end, he chose conducting, having heard Carlos Kleiber's father, Erich, conduct *Beethoven's Symphony No. 5* when Solti was only 14. His conducting debut in Budapest on 12 March, 1938, coincided with the Nazi Anschluss (his father had changed the family name to avoid anti-semitism) and Solti left Hungary for Switzerland. Post-war jobs with the Munich State Opera and in Frankfurt were followed by a golden period at the Royal Opera House, Covent Garden, in the 1960s, followed by an immensely successful Music Directorship of the Chicago Symphony Orchestra. His exuberant, demonstrative style on the podium has been preserved in more than 250 recordings. He died in September 1997, by which time he was Sir Georg Solti, a British citizen.

SONATA

The word 'sonata' means 'sounded' or 'played' and is the opposite of 'cantata', meaning 'sung'. It is a piece for either a solo instrumentalist (very often a pianist), a soloist with piano accompaniment (or occasionally a small ensemble). Today's interpretation of a sonata is largely that which was prevalent during the Classical and Romantic periods. Sonata form – the rules by which a sonata is written – can also be applied to other genres, though: many symphonies have a movement which, while not being a sonata, is written in sonata form. A standard Classical or Romantic sonata has three movements, usually – but not always – one quick, one slow and another quick. The rules of sonata form dictate three sections within each movement: an exposition, containing the main big tunes; a development, in which the tunes from the exposition are built on and varied; and finally a recapitulation, where themes from the exposition return.

SOUSA, JOHN PHILIP
1854-1932

Sousa was born in Washington DC to a family of Portuguese descent. From singing and violin-playing during his childhood, Sousa moved via theatre orchestras to directing first the Marine Band and then his own group of musicians. From the age of 38, he toured his band with amazing success across the USA, Europe and much of the rest of the world (wherever you are in the UK, you are never very far from a former Sousa concert date). Sousa composed more than 130 marches, becoming known as 'The March King' and creating his own marching bass brass instrument, the Sousaphone, in the process. He wrote his *Stars and Stripes Forever* on Christmas Day, 1896, and played it at pretty much every concert he gave for the next 36 years of his life. By the time he died in 1932, it had become the USA's national march.

† **Recommended Listening:**
  The Washington Post

SPOHR, LOUIS
1784-1859

Spohr was a violin prodigy, who became one of the most successful composers of his day. Born in Braunschweig, he soon outgrew infant prodigy status to tour Russia and Germany as both violinist and conductor. As well as a successful stint as leader of the Theater an der Wien Orchestra in Vienna, several visits to the UK (at the behest of the Royal Philharmonic Society) not only made him famous but also prompted the vogue for conducting with a baton, which has been standard practice ever since. Spohr spent the last 37 years of his life in Kassel (midway between Dortmund and Leipzig) conducting, still writing and championing Wagner. Alongside the popularisation of the baton among conductors, he is also credited with the introduction of the chin-rest for violinists.

† **Recommended Listening:**
  Octet

STANFORD, CHARLES VILLIERS
1852-1924

Though he now largely forgotten, it is a mark of the esteem in which Sir Charles Villiers Stanford was held in his day that he was buried in Westminster Abbey, next to Henry Purcell. He was born in Dublin in 1852 and was educated there and at Queen's College, Cambridge, where, at his father's insistence, he read classics rather than music. Nevertheless, it was his time in Cambridge – he conducted the Music Society orchestra and became organist at Trinity College while still an undergraduate – that put him firmly on the musical map.

After further study in Germany, Stanford began composing in earnest. His prodigious musical output includes seven symphonies, ten operas, 15 concertos, chamber, piano and organ pieces, songs and more than 30 large-scale choral works. However, it was his role as Composition

Professor at the then new Royal College of Music that enabled him to leave a real mark on musical posterity.

† **Recommended Listening:**

Magnificat In G

STANLEY, JOHN

1712-1786

John Stanley was an English composer, born in London in 1712, who was blind from the age of two, following a fall. He was taught the organ by Maurice Green, organist at St. Paul's Cathedral, and soon was playing in his own church, aged just 11. When he was 17, he became the youngest ever music graduate from Oxford University. Aged 22, he was made organist at the Temple Church, a job he held for the rest of his life, becoming a composing and performing phenomenon – his organ voluntaries were famous. When he was 48, upon Handel's death, it was Stanley who continued the oratorio tradition at Covent Garden.

† **Recommended Listening:**

Trumpet Voluntary in D Op. 6 No. 5

STRAUSS FAMILY

The Strauss Family is dominated by one man – Johann Strauss Junior – whose reputation overshadowed that of his father, and of his younger brothers. In the fiercely fought battleground for musical supremacy as master of the Viennese waltz, father and son ran rival orchestras. When his brother Eduard Strauss set up his own orchestra, there were three.

Johann Strauss Sr. A proficient violinist and viola player, who became the founding father of the Strauss dynasty. He formed his own band when he was just 22 years old, after playing in those of the composer Josef Lanner. Strauss was eventually booked at the Sperl Ballroom in Vienna, where he became famous. He also played for the court balls.

Despite composing a couple of hundred waltzes, he would eventually be eclipsed by his son, and remembered, pretty much, for one work: the *Radetzky March*.

Johann Strauss Jr. Despite being a composer and conductor himself, Johann Strauss Sr. forbade his son to follow in his footsteps. As a result, Johann Strauss Jr. became a bank clerk, learning music in secret. Eventually, he set up his own orchestra (aged just 19) in opposition to his father. Upon his father's death, he merged both bands and became famous for his waltzes (nearly 400 of them). Spotting the potential of the stage, he switched to operetta when he was 56; his greatest one, *Die Fledermaus (The Bat)*, is a staple of the operatic repertoire. He could count Brahms, Wagner and even Schoenberg amongst his fans.

Josef and Eduard Strauss The brothers of Johann Strauss Jr. were by no means the leading lights of the Strauss family, but they did perform an important role in keeping the tradition going. Josef deputised as conductor of the band and had a hand in the composition of the *Pizzicato Polka*, with his elder brother Johann. Eduard took over the band in 1872, and brought it to the UK. A polka specialist rather than a waltz king, he is also the brother responsible for burning all the original manuscripts of the entire Strauss clan, which is why we have some works only in piano versions available to this day.

† **Recommended Listening:**

By The Beautiful Blue Danube by *Johann Strauss Jr.*

Strauss, Richard
1864-1949

The son of the principal horn player in the Munich Court Orchestra (now the Bavarian State Orchestra), Strauss grew up a Wagner lover – a predilection possibly stimulated by his father's antipathy towards Wagner's music. Having written his first symphony at the age of 16 without any formal composition lessons, he soon became regarded as a musical iconoclast, first as a conductor and then as a composer. His series of symphonic tone poems, starting with *Tod und Verklarung* (*Death and Transfiguration*) and *Macbeth*, continuing with *Also Sprach Zarathustra*, *Don Juan*, *Ein Heldenleben* and *Till Eulenspiegel* made him the hottest musical property in Germany.

With the 20th century, Strauss turned to opera, becoming, arguably, the most important operatic composer of his generation. *Salome*, which created a scandal at its first performances because of its Biblical theme, *Elektra* and *Der Rosenkavalier* are towering works, still firmly in the operatic repertoire. His *Four Last Songs* for soprano and orchestra (there were to be five, but the cycle was left incomplete) is one of the most moving swansongs ever produced by any composer.

† **Recommended Listening:**
Also Sprach Zarathustra

STRAVINSKY, IGOR
1882-1971

Stravinsky was one of the most influential and enigmatically charming composers of the 20th century. His composing life is often divided into distinct periods, in much the same way as that of the artist Picasso. For Picasso's blue, cubist and surrealist periods, substitute for Stravinsky, Russian, Neo-Classical and Serial.

Stravinsky's three great ballets, *Firebird*, *Petrushka* and *The Rite of Spring* all belong to his Russian period, with their use of native folksong or folk-like motifs. The masterpieces of his Neo-Classical period, where he rediscovered classic forms, are the *Symphony of Psalms*, *Symphony in C* and the *Symphony in Three Movements*.

In the 1950s and 1960s, he adopted Schoenberg's 12 tone techniques to produced works like the ballet *Agon* and the choral and orchestral work *Canticum Sacrum*. Across his long life, he furnished quotation books with many of their best lines, including the classic 'Harpists spend 90% of their time tuning their harps, and the other 10% playing out of tune'.

† **Recommended Listening:**
The Dance of the Princesses from *The Firebird*

SUITE

A suite is a collection of instrumental pieces intended to be played together at one sitting. The original French meaning of suite is 'things that follow', so therefore it came to mean music that was played in succession. Over the years it has varied in make-up. A Baroque suite has several movements, almost always featuring an Allemande, Sarabande, Gigue and Courante. It often also included any number of variations of the following: Gavotte, Minuet, Passepied and Rigaudon. Each style of movement has its own, often dance-derived, rules.

Later, with the symphony replacing the suite in popularity, it became common to use the suite as a means of gathering together a composer's best moments from an opera or play, sometimes to prevent them slipping into obscurity if the stage work they came from flopped. Sometimes, this job was done by other composers: as in the case of Bizet's two *Carmen* suites.

SULLIVAN, ARTHUR
1842-1900

In 1869, the 33-year-old W.S. Gilbert, previously a lawyer but now a writer and a dramatist, was introduced to a 27-year old budding composer, Arthur Sullivan – a man who already had his *Irish Symphony* and *Overture in C* under his belt. Nothing much came of the meeting at first; *Thespis*, the first piece they wrote together, was a relative failure. Then the young impresario Richard D'Oyly Carte commissioned the partnership to produce a supporting piece for his production of *Offenbach's La Perichole*. The result, *Trial by Jury*, was a riotous success.

It was the first of the so-called 'Savoy Operas,' named after the theatre built by D'Oyly Carte in which Gilbert and Sullivan flourished (the first to be lit completely by electric light). By 1890, the relationship had ruptured. Though the two men got together again to produce two more operettas, neither was a success.

THE MIKADO (1885)

This comeback opera following the less successful *Princess Ida* gave the Gilbert and Sullivan partnership their longest ever run of 672 performances. It ran in London and New York and eventually transferred to Vienna and Berlin, where hits such as *A Wand'ring Minstrel, I* and *Three Little Maids from School are We* were greeted with rave reviews, before the show moved on to France, Holland, Hungary, Spain, Belgium, Germany and Russia. This helps to give some sense of the scale of the Gilbert and Sullivan phenomenon that made both men (and Richard D'Oyly Carte) very wealthy.

SUPPÉ, FRANZ VON
1819-1895

Born in the then Dalmatian city of Spoleto (now Split in Croatia), von Suppé's musical talent was first spotted by the local bandmaster and choirmaster. When he moved to Vienna, aged 16, he was determined to study music, despite false starts in law and medicine. He soon became not only an opera conductor but also a singer, composing a huge number of stage works along the way and becoming a rival to Johann Strauss Jr. for the title of the Viennese Offenbach. However, the overtures to his operettas *Poet and Peasant* and *Morning, Noon and Night in Vienna* fare better these days than do the operas themselves.

† **Recommended Listening:**
  Overture to *Light Cavalry*

Symphony

The word symphony derives from Greek, meaning 'a sounding together'. There have been various definitions of what exactly a symphony is over the years, but today it means an extended work for an orchestra. Very often, but not always, this consists of four movements; many consider it the purest musical form a composer can write.

FIVE GREAT SYMPHONIES:

Haydn: *Symphony No. 45* **(1772)** Haydn is considered the 'father of the symphony', composing a total of 104 of them through his career. *Symphony No. 45*, nicknamed '*The Farewell*', sees Haydn writing his players off the stage, one by one, at the end. It was a hint to his employer that his musicians were overworked and wanted to go home to see their families.

Mozart: *Symphony No. 41* **(1788)** Nicknamed the '*Jupiter*' – though not by the composer – Mozart's last symphony is a masterly summation of all his musical experience and skill.

Beethoven: *Symphony No. 9* **(1824)** Considered by many to be the finest symphony ever, Beethoven's late masterpiece was written when the composer was completely deaf. It incorporates a choral setting of Friedrich Schiller's *Ode to Joy*.

Mahler: *Symphony No. 5* **(1902)** From the opening solo trumpet call, through the incredibly moving fourth movement Adagietto to its galloping Rondo Finale, this is symphonic writing in its purest form.

Sibelius: *Symphony No. 5* **(1915)** Sibelius conducted the premiere of this much-loved symphony on his 50th birthday. The famous repeated horn motif in the final movement is said to have been inspired by swan calls and has since been borrowed by everyone from John Coltrane to Strawberry Switchblade.

T

TALLIS, THOMAS
c.1505-1585

The details of Thomas Tallis's childhood are lost in the mists of time, but we do know that, by his forties, he was first a Gentleman and then organist of the Chapel Royal. In partnership with William Byrd – with whom he shared the position of organist – he was granted the exclusive licence by Elizabeth I to print music. Despite the apparent value of the licence, they failed to make much money out of the venture and were forced to go cap in hand to the Queen to rescue them financially. Known for his church music in general, such as his *Mass for Four Voices* and his *Lamentations*, the staggeringly beautiful *Spem in Alium* is possibly Tallis's most breathtaking work, an amazingly skilful combination of 40 separate vocal entries.

† **Recommended Listening:**
   Spem in Alium

TARTINI, GIUSEPPE
1692-1770

Born in what was then part of northern Italy but is now Slovenia, Tartini intended to become a monk, but he had to rethink this after eloping with the bishop's daughter while studying theology at Padua University. Having married, the couple evaded the bishop's arrest warrant for three years, before Tartini was forced to leave town and his wife was sent to a convent. The composer took the opportunity to hole himself away in a monastery and perfect his amazing violin technique, returning to Padua, now pardoned, and staying there as head of the Cappello del Santo for the rest of his life. His compositions naturally reflect his supremacy as a violinist.

† **Recommended Listening:**
 Sonata for solo violin, 'The Devil's Trill'

Tavener, John
1944-

Sir John Tavener was a classmate of fellow composer John Rutter at Highgate School. His early school compositions were instrumental in winning him a scholarship to the Royal Academy of Music when he was 18. Here he met and was influenced by Stravinsky (who, it is said, read through the score of his *John Donne Sonnets* and simply wrote 'I know!' on the first page). His early student oratorio, *The Whale* (1966) won him a wider audience when it was recorded by The Beatles' Apple record label. Aged 34, he joined the Russian Orthodox Church and much of his subsequent music, such as the *Liturgy of St. John Chrysostom*, reflects this faith. From 2000 onwards, he broadened his religious and musical scope; his *Requiem* (2009) sets Sanskrit, Hebrew and Islamic texts alongside the traditional Latin.

† **Recommended Listening:**
 The Lamb

Tchaikovsky, Pyotr Il'ych
1840-1893

Tchaikovsky's prolifically tuneful brand of palatable Russian nationalism constitutes possibly the most exportable form of his country's music over the last three centuries. He was born some 600 miles east of Moscow in Votkinsk, an industrial town in the Ural Mountains, where his father was the manager of the local ironworks.

Like many composers before him (particularly Russian ones), he eschewed music at first, studying law and then entering the civil service as a clerk in the Ministry of Justice, before finally turning to music when the composer Rubinstein founded the St. Petersburg Conservatoire in 1863.

Aged 28, Tchaikovsky came into contact with the Russian nationalists (Rimksy-Korsakov and the 'Mighty Handful'), but he was always somewhat removed from them: as infused as it was with his country's heritage, his music is plainly identifiable as pure Tchaikovsky rather anything else. By the time he was in his thirties, he was well-known enough to come to the attention of one Nadezhda von Meck, a canny businesswoman who had been the driving force behind her husband's railroad engineering company. For 13 years, she funded Tchaikovsky – on the strict stipulation that they never met.

During this time, Tchaikovsky rose to fame in Russia and beyond. By the time the relationship ended, he had already written masterpieces such as the opera *Eugene Onegin* and the ballet *The Sleeping Beauty*. He had also completed five of his symphonies. He toured the USA in the early 1890s, where he was the star conductor at the opening of the new Carnegie Hall in 1891. He visited England to receive an honorary degree from Cambridge University in 1893, producing the ever popular *Nutcracker* between the two trips.

Despite these successes, life was not easy for Tchaikovsky. He suffered badly from bouts of acute depression, not least because of the need to conceal the fact that he was homosexual. His sudden death, four days after the premiere of his *Symphony No. 6* in November 1893, has given rise to various conspiracy theories. One Russian criminal forensic expert has argued that Tchaikovsky was forced to commit suicide by a secret cabal of his former law colleagues and that his death was covered up by being attributed to cholera.

† **Recommended Listening:**
1812 Overture

TELEMANN, GEORG PHILIP
1681-1767

One of the most prolific composers ever, Telemann wrote masses of music for more or less every instrumental or vocal combination. He studied law at Leipzig University, following his parents' wishes, but soon switched to music, winning church posts in Leipzig, Eisenach, Frankfurt and Hamburg. At the age of 41, he turned down the offer of a return to Leipzig; the post he rejected was subsequently filled by 37-year-old second choice, J.S. Bach. Living to a grand old age, Telemann remained active as a composer into his eighties, a feat made possible by a team of copyists and occasional visits to take the waters at various health spas. His massive catalogue of works was dispersed to various rural libraries in Germany during the Second World War, to avoid destruction.

† **Recommended Listening:**
Overture in F Major

TONE POEM

Also known as the symphonic poem, 'tone poem' was first coined by the composer Liszt to denote a symphonic work, very often in just one movement, which seeks to portray a descriptive subject. Liszt's tone poems generally took various literary or mythological figures as their subject – *Mazeppa*, *Hamlet* and *Orpheus* were three typical examples. While later composers followed the same path, they also ventured into new, less definite fields. Delius's *On Hearing the First Cuckoo in Spring* is a tone poem, but one depicting an almost Impressionistic mood, rather than a specific narrative picture. Richard Strauss made something of a speciality of tone poems, with works such as *Don Juan*, *Till Eulenspiegel*, Ein Heldenleben and *Also Sprach Zarathustra*; the *Sunrise* section of *Also Sprach Zarathustra* was used as the opening theme for the cult science-fiction movie *2001: A Space Odyssey*.

TRANSCRIPTION

A transcription is an interpretative paraphrasing by one composer of another composer's original work, or part of it. It developed out of the penchant for producing 'opera fantasies', usually piano-based works which take two or more of the themes from a certain opera, and develop them further, and together, in a new piece by a different composer.

Liszt was the first real master of the piano transcription, composing more than 50. To be able to play these pieces well, it helps to possess the phenomenal performance technique that Liszt himself enjoyed. Busoni continued the tradition into the 20th century with his Bach paraphrases.

TROMBONE

Descended from an early English instrument called the 'shagbolt' (or sackbut), the trombone is a length of brass tubing whose notes are changed by lengthening the tube with a slide. Mozart used trombones to great effect in his opera *Don Giovanni*, but their first ever use in a symphony came about when Beethoven chose to include them in his *Symphony No. 5*. They possess a stout and, let's not deny it, loud sound, useful for its ability to penetrate, but equally at home in a proud, perhaps tragic mode, such as in the *Tuba Mirum* from Mozart's *Requiem*.

TRUMPET

To call the trumpet a lip-vibrated, cylindrical bore aerophone, while being technically accurate, would not begin to convey the impressive range of colours that it can produce. This is an instrument which can range from attention-grabbing authority to haunting, elegiac beauty. The modern trumpet, most commonly in B flat (which means all its music is written one whole tone above where it sounds) is the undisputed leader of the brass section, a full eight feet of coiled tubing, whose every note is produced via just three valves and the ever-changing lipwork (called embouchure) of the player's mouth.

Great Trumpet Concertos

Haydn: A case of right place, right time for Haydn. His friend, Weidinger, had just developed the trumpet with valves (previously it had been what is termed a 'natural trumpet' whose notes and agility was limited by what could be achieved simply by the player's lips).

Hummel: Hummel wrote his *Trumpet Concerto* when he succeeded Haydn at the Esterházy for the same trumpet virtuoso and inventor, Weidinger.

Arutunian: A much later 20th century work, it is a testament to the calibre of this Armenian composer's concerto that it has become a trumpet audition staple so quickly.

TRUMPET VOLUNTARY

Many bridegrooms have had the hairs on the back of their necks raised in a mixture of apprehension and relief at the start of a rousing trumpet voluntary. Despite originally being organ pieces (which made a feature out of using the trumpet stop) they are very often used, arranged for trumpet or not, to signal the bride's arrival and hopefully elegant procession down the aisle.

Tuba

This benevolent-sounding bass brass instrument comprises a cup-shaped mouthpiece, around 18 feet of coiled tubing and, usually, four valves (there can be anything from three to six). Despite being principally a bass instrument – it can reach nearly an octave lower than the standard bass singing voice – it also possesses an impressive upper register stretching into the high male tenor range. This versatility has made it an extremely useful instrument for composers since its introduction in around 1835. Vaughan Williams wrote his *Tuba Concerto* in 1954 for the London Symphony Orchestra's then principal tuba, Philip Catelinet. It soon became one of the composer's surprise hits.

U

UNGAR, JAY
1946-

Born in New York to Hungarian immigrant parents, Jay Ungar's Greenwich Village upbringing may seem a million miles from the Catskill strains of his famous hit tune, *The Ashokan Farewell*. In actual fact, the moving melody, originally a country waltz, was written for fond-felt final nights at his annual Fiddle and Dance Camp, run out of the Ashokan Campus of New York State University. It came to prominence after being used in Ken Burn's television films *The Civil War*, and its arrangement by Captain J.R. Perkins, then of The Band of Her Majesty's Royal Marines, propelled it to the higher echelons of the Classic FM Hall of Fame.

V

VARIATIONS

The musical form of 'theme and variations' is one in which a theme (original or borrowed from another composer) is subjected to a series of self-contained new interpretations or 'variations'. There are no hard and fast rules about the number of variations or the exact form which they take, with the decision on this resting with the composer of the new work. Possibly the most famous set of theme and variations are Elgar's so-called *Enigma Variations* (more properly known as *Variations on an Original Theme*). This is due to the mystery left behind about the nature of the original tune itself and also because of the puzzle surrounding the people alluded to in each of the variations' titles. The latter has long been solved, but the former continues to exercise musical brains. Another favourite is Rachmaninov's *Rhapsody on a Theme of Paganini*. Part piano concerto, part variations, yet called a rhapsody, this set of 24 re-workings of a tune borrowed from Paganini reaches its highpoint in *Variation 18*, when the composer turns both the world and the original tune upside down to produce three minutes of musical heaven.

VAUGHAN WILLIAMS, RALPH
1872-1958

A great landscape painter who worked in tones and semitones rather than oils or watercolours, Vaughan Williams was born in the Gloucestershire village of Down Ampney, but went to school at Charterhouse, where he was in the orchestra. Having composed from early on, he went early to the Royal College of Music, and then Cambridge, before returning to the RCM, where Holst was a fellow student. He then had lessons, albeit briefly, with Bruch in Berlin.

Shortly after the turn of the 20th century, Vaughan Williams became hooked on folk song collecting, alongside Cecil Sharp, Percy Grainger and others, and was responsible for the survival of numerous folk gems. Following more time studying, this time with Ravel in Paris, he returned to England to write *On Wenlock Edge* and incidental music to *The Wasps* (for a Cambridge student production). This was also the time of successes such as *Fantasia on a Theme of Thomas Tallis* and *A London Symphony*.

Vaughan Williams went on to live through the two world wars – he was a stretcher bearer in the first, but a respected veteran composer during the second – and came to be regarded as one of Britain's finest symphonic writers. A late crop of works in the late 1940s and early 1950s underlined his pre-eminence. He was a familiar figure at his famous White Gates house in Dorking (where you will find his statue).

† **Recommended Listening:**
　The Lark Ascending

VERDI, GIUSEPPE
1813-1901

Born near Busseto in Parma, Verdi showed musical promise very early; by the time he was seven, he was already helping the organist at the local church. Though he was turned down for a place at the Milan Conservatory because of his youth, he persuaded Vincenzo Lavigra, a Milanese composer, to give him private composition lessons. Antonio Baressi, a well-to-do grocer who had befriended the impoverished would-be composer, paid for them. On his return to Busseto to become the local music director, Verdi married Baressi's beautiful daughter.

Verdi was always determined to succeed as an opera composer. Things went well for him at the start – *Oberto*, his first opera, was a success – but then tragedy struck. His two young children perished in quick succession.

Then, his wife died of a brain fever while he was struggling against the clock to finish *Un Giorno di Regno* (*King for a Day*). It was his first attempt at a comic opera and it was booed off the stage at its premiere. The grief-stricken Verdi decided to abandon composing as a result.

Luckily, La Scala, Milan's great opera house, came to the rescue. Bartolomeo Merelli, its director, sent him the libretto for *Nabucco*. Inspired by the story, Verdi started to compose again. The opera was a huge success, winning him an international reputation. What he later referred to as his 'galley years' followed, as opera after opera poured from his pen. Though its story got him into trouble with the censors, *Rigoletto* was a smash hit, as was *Il Trovatore*. By contrast, *La Traviata* was a failure when it was first performed, probably because the audience at its Venice premiere did not like the plot.

There was no stopping Verdi, however. Over the following years, his operas – especially the ones, such as *Don Carlos*, which he wrote for Paris and La Forza del Destino, which he composed for St. Petersburg – became grander and grander. Now rich and successful, he married Giuseppina Strepponi, an opera singer who had been his long-time mistress and set up home with her on the country estate he purchased outside Busseto. He had reached a height of popularity unequalled by an Italian composer before or since.

Verdi continued to compose great operas, his style developing and becoming more refined over the years. After he had written *Aida*, he again decided to give opera up until Arrigo Boito, a young fellow-composer and librettist, and Giulio Ricordi, his publisher, persuaded him to write *Otello*. It was his second stab at setting Shakespeare – he had composed *Macbeth* many years before – but this time the result was a triumph. Special newspaper correspondents from all over Europe flocked to Milan to witness the premiere; the young Arturo Toscanini, later to be hailed as one of the greatest Verdi conductors ever, played cello in the orchestra.

Falstaff, Verdi's very last opera, followed in 1893. Boito again provided the libretto, which he based on Shakespeare's *The Merry Wives*

of Windsor. It is a comic opera masterpiece. After it, with the exception of his *Four Sacred Pieces*, Verdi wrote no more. When he finally died, some 28,000 people lined the streets of Milan for his funeral.

† **Recommended Listening:**

 Quartet from *Rigoletto*

VIENNA PHILHARMONIC ORCHESTRA

Formed in 1842 by the composer Otto Nicolai, the Vienna Philharmonic is one of Europe's supreme orchestras. Its founding principles of autonomy and democracy still hold true today. It selects its own conductors and its players are all chosen from the Vienna State Opera orchestra. The Vienna Philharmonic is resident at Vienna's amazing, gilded Musikverein concert hall and its seasons are often oversubscribed. Booking for the famous New Year's Day concert have to be made sometimes a couple of years in advance. The orchestra has been directed by an illustrious line of great conductors, including Gustav Mahler, Wilhelm Furtwängler and Herbert von Karajan.

VILLA-LOBOS, HEITOR
1887-1959

Born in Rio de Janeiro, Villa-Lobos studied music with his father until he was 12 years old, at which point he became a guitarist in a Brazilian street band – something he would later commemorate in his *Chôros*. From 16 onwards, he made money playing cello in a theatre orchestra, but also began to study his country's folk music. He was funded by the government to study in Paris, returning as a music educator and composer when he was 43; he founded the Brazilian Academy of Music. For the last two decades of his life, he benefited from the championship of the conductor Leopold Stokowski, who was instrumental in bringing his music to a wider audience. Today his most enduring works outside his home country are his *Bachaianas Brasileiras*, a fusion of Bach and Brazil.

VIOLA

If the stringed instruments of the orchestra were singers (soprano at the top followed by alto, tenor and bass), the viola would be the alto. Born at roughly the same time as the violin, it has a more mellow, burnished tone than its counterpart. With its four strings – tuned to C, G, D and A, five notes below the violin – it has been less favoured by composers in terms of concertos, but there is a fine body of work for it. Berlioz's *Harold in Italy* was commissioned by Paganini as a concerto for viola – the instrument was his passion at the time. Walton's *Viola Concerto* was premiered in 1929 by composer Paul Hindemith, a concert violist.

VIOLIN

The crowned king of string instruments, the violins make up a third of the modern orchestra, the largest of any section. The violin has a fantastic range of around four octaves and is capable of amazing agility. It was developed, in the way we know it today, in Italy in the 16th century and enjoyed a golden period in the 17th century, a situation that gives rise to the deified status of violins of the time, notably those made by Stradivari.

FOUR BEAUS OF THE VIOLIN WORLD

Stradivari: often known by the Latin version of his name (Stradivarius) Antonio Stradivari is considered the greatest violin-maker. Known as 'Strads' and prized for their amazing tone (particularly those made from 1698 to 1725), Strads sell for art world prices. In 2006, Christie's sold a Stradivarius, nicknamed 'The Hammer', for $3.54 million.

Guarneri: a family of violin makers (the technical term is luthiers) who, like Stradivari, worked out of Cremona in the 17th and early 18th centuries. In 2008, Sotheby's sold a Guerneri, previously owned by the composer Vieuxtemps, for 'well in excess' of The Hammer's previous record.

Amati: the earliest of the great violin makers. Andrea, family head and founder of the Cremona school of violin making, is thought to have given the modern violin its style. One of his pupils was said to be Stradivari.

Montagnana: sometimes known as 'the Mighty Venetian', Domenico Montagana is also famed for his cellos. He worked from a small shop close to the Rialto Bridge in Venice.

VIVALDI, ANTONIO
1678-1741

At the stage in musical history when J.S. Bach was composing in Germany, Handel was making music in England and Couperin was writing in France, Vivaldi was doing the same in Italy. The composer of *The Four Seasons* was born in Venice, a sickly child of a violinist in the St Mark's Orchestra. He learned the violin in childhood, accompanying his father on some of his musical trips. When he was 15 years old, he began studying for the priesthood, being ordained ten years later. He frequently applied the initials LD – Laus Deo or Praise be to God – to his scores.

The same year, Vivaldi joined the La Pieta orphans institute as head of the violins – the orphanage had an impressive orchestra and chorus – remaining there, on and off, in various posts until he was 38. During this time that he wrote many great instrumental works, including his now famous concertos and sonatas. Between the ages of 38 and 50, he worked variously out of Mantua and Rome, concentrating on opera, although he still composed 'by post' for La Pieta. He then ventured further afield – to Vienna and Prague – before returning to La Pieta as Maestro di Capella.

Vivaldi soon lost the job because his desire to travel got him into trouble with his Venetian employers. Late in life, he moved to Vienna in search of more opera commissions, only to be thwarted by the death of the Emperor Charles VI and the ensuing, customary closure of all the opera houses during the official period of court mourning. He died, aged 63, in relative poverty and was buried in the Hospital Burial Ground.

† **Recommended Listening:**

The Four Seasons

WAGNER, RICHARD
1813-1883

Like him or loathe him, there is no disputing the fact that Wagner was a colossus among composers. Through his operas, he revolutionised music, notably by pushing the boundaries of harmony to their limits and through his use of *leitmotivs* – recurring musical mottos associated with a particular character, place or even an idea – in his compositions. He called what he wrote 'the music of the future'. His enemies condemned it as unsingable and unplayable, dismissing the sound of singers and the enormous Wagner orchestra in full cry as no more than an ugly cacophony.

Obsessed with opera from the start, Wagner was given lessons in his mid-teens by a leading Leipzig music-teacher before entering the celebrated Thomasschule, where J.S. Bach had been Kantor more than a century before, and going on to university. Then, he started about making his living. He took various conducting jobs at Wurzburg, Magdeburg and then in Riga. Forced to flee from his creditors, he took refuge in Paris, where he wrote the operas *Rienzi* and *The Flying Dutchman*. Successful productions of both works in Dresden a few years later brought him instant fame, as did *Tannhäuser*, which soon followed.

Wagner's good fortune soon ran out. He left Germany to escape arrest following his involvement in the unsuccessful 1849 revolution, finally ending up in Switzerland. It was there that he wrote not only *The Rhinegold* and *The Valkyrie* (the first two operas of the mammoth *Ring cycle*), but *Tristan and Isolde* into the bargain. Yet his compositions seemed as far away as ever from winning him the acclaim which he craved. When a revised version of *Tannhäuser* was put on by the Paris Opera, it was literally booed off the stage. It did not help that his operas cost a fortune to stage. It seemed as if Wagner might well go down in musical history as an impossible-to-perform composer.

Then, Wagner's luck turned again. He was taken up by King Ludwig of Bavaria, who paid for the production of *The Rhinegold*, *The Valkyrie* and *The Mastersingers of Nuremberg* (Wagner's only semi-comical opera) and helped the composer raise the money he needed to build his own opera house at Bayreuth. The first performance of the now complete Ring cycle (*The Rhinegold*, *The Valkyrie*, *Siegfried* and *The Twilight of the Gods*) took place there in 1876, with Hans Richter conducting but Wagner backseat-driving every last detail. He completed *Parsifal*, his last opera, in 1882, by which time he was seriously ill with angina. He died of a heart attack while recuperating in Venice, and was buried in the grounds of his Bayreuth villa.

Wagner's stormy career ended in triumph, but, for much of it, he was his own worst enemy. His extravagance meant that he was always short of funds, often spending as much time dodging his creditors as he did composing. Nor were his personal relationships better conducted. Convinced of his own destiny, he possessed deeply unpleasant views and was racist, egotistical and often completely amoral. But, unpalatable though such views were and are, there is no gainsaying the undeniable beauty, power and sheer grandeur of his best work.

† **Recommended Listening:**

Prelude and *Liebestod* from *Tristan and Isolde*

WALTON, WILLIAM
1902-1983

Although musical, William Walton's parents were not well off. Aged ten, he won a choral scholarship to Christ Church Cathedral School, Oxford, where his early aspirations to become a composer were fostered. Despite eventually failing his degree, Walton met the poets Edith Sitwell and Siegfried Sassoon while an undergraduate, later becoming part of their London social set.

Having explored the mixing of classical music and jazz in works like *Façade* and also having composed his *Symphony No. 1* and choral pieces such as *Belshazzar's Feast*, Walton was excused military service in the Second World War in order to continue to compose. Patriotic scores, such as his *Spitfire Prelude and Fugue* and his music for Olivier's film of *Henry V*, were the result. After the war, he moved to Ischia, an island off the Italian coast, where he concentrated on operas, such as *Troilus and Cressida*. Thankfully, his temporary post-war reputation of being old fashioned has been re-assessed since his death in 1983.

† **Recommended Listening:**

Crown Imperial

WARLOCK, PETER
1894-1930

Although born in London, Philip Heseltine moved to Wales with his mother at an early age. He went to Eton, but further study at Oxford and then University College London lasted just a year and a term respectively. Both during and after a stay in Ireland when he was 23, he began composing, under the name Peter Warlock (he still used his real name for other work, such as his job as music critic of the Daily Mail). He lived a riotous life for a time in Eynsford, Kent, with the composer Moeran, before moving back to London in 1928. After a creatively fruitless period, including bouts of unemployment and depression, he was found dead from gas poisoning in his flat. His most enduring work, the *Capriol Suite*, comes from his apparently drunken, but productive, three years in Eynsford.

† **Recommended Listening:**

Capriol Suite

WEBER, CARL MARIA VON
1786-1826

It is easy to see how, with a father who was both a musician and theatrical impresario, Weber was always going to be obsessed by the world of opera. He was taught by Haydn's brother, Michael, in Salzburg and also studied for a time in Vienna. A productive period in Stuttgart was halted by seemingly false charges of financial fraud, whereupon he embarked on a period of short-term conducting jobs in Darmstadt, Munich, Prague and Dresden.

It was in Dresden that Weber wrote the opera *Der Freischütz*, which made him an overnight sensation in Germany. It established a new breed of German opera which was to prove influential for years to come. *Euryanthe* followed, but it was while rehearsing his *Oberon* for its premiere at Covent Garden that he died in London, from tuberculosis, aged just 39. His two concertos and a concertino for the clarinet are among his most popular works today.

† **Recommended Listening:**
Clarinet Concerto No.1

WELSH NATIONAL OPERA

Founded thanks to the efforts of a group of miners, doctors, teachers, shop assistants and steel workers in 1943, WNO performed its first ever operas, a double-bill of *Cavalleria Rusticana* and *Pagliacci*, three years later. It is now recognised as one of the most innovative opera companies in the world. An early reputation for performing rare Verdi operas preceded touring seasons in Swansea, Bristol, Birmingham and beyond, alongside the Welsh Philharmonia, which was renamed the Orchestra of Welsh National Opera in 1979.

WIDOR, CHARLES-MARIE
1844-1937

Living to a ripe old age meant that while Widor's early memories might well have been of the Revolution of 1848, he was still around to witness Franklin D. Roosevelt's second term in office, more than 90 years later. The son of an organ builder, he studied with his father and later in Brussels before landing one of the most prestigious posts in France – organist at St. Sulpice, Paris.

Later, as organ and then composition professor at the Paris Conservatoire, Widor devoted his efforts to furthering the cause of the organ in music. His greatest legacy is his body of ten symphonies for the solo organ, in which he put the instrument through its paces, keen to show that it was capable of emulating the entire orchestra.

† **Recommended Listening:**
  Toccata

WOLF-FERRARI, ERMANNO
1876-1948

Born Ermanno Wolf in Venice, Wolf-Ferrari divided his time between music and art as a boy, choosing first to follow in the footsteps of his artist father and study painting at Rome's Academia di Belle Arte. He switched to music having moved to Munich when he was 17 years old, studying for a time with the composer Boito.

Seemingly, Wolf-Ferrari was more appreciated in Germany than in Italy, certainly during his lifetime. He spent the First World War years in Switzerland, composing little – a silence he only broke when he was in his 40s. When he was 63, he was made professor of composition at the prestigious Mozarteum in Salzburg. He died in his native Venice, aged 72.

† **Recommended Listening:**
  The Secret Of Susanna: Intermezzo

Z

ZIPOLI, DOMENICO
1688-1726

Domenico Zipoli was an organist, choirmaster and composer – or at least he was for the first 28 years of his short life. Born in Prato near Florence, where he studied, he began his successful career as a composer there, later working in Milan and Rome. Then, in 1716, he became a Jesuit missionary, sailing to Córdoba, Argentina, where he spent three years studying theology. He was part of the same so-called 'Jesuit Reductions' – an attempt to convert the local tribes to Christianity – which featured in the 1986 Roland Joffé movie *The Mission* (in which Father Gabriel soothes the locals with his exquisite oboe playing). As well as his magnum opus – a collection of sonatas, which he wrote in 1716 – his popularity blossomed from the early 1990s onwards with the revival of his *Elevazione*, a piece for oboe and strings he wrote to mark the raising of the Host during Mass.

† **Recommended Listening:**
Elevazione